W9-CNK-638

THE COUNCIL OF CHIEF STATE SCHOOL OFFICERS

The Council of Chief State School Officers (CCSSO) is a nonpartisan, nationwide, nonprofit organization
of public officials who head departments of elementary and secondary education in the states, the
District of Columbia, the Department of Defense Education Activity, and five U.S. extra-state jurisdictions.
CCSSO provides leadership, advocacy, and technical assistance on major educational issues.
The Council seeks member consensus on major educational issues and expresses their views
to civic and professional organizations, federal agencies, Congress, and the public.

Council of Chief State School Officers
One Massachusetts Avenue, NW, Suite 700
Washington, DC 20001-1431
Phone (202) 336-7000
Fax (202) 408-8072
www.ccsso.org

Recommended Citation:

Olson, J., and Fremer, J. (2013). *TILSA Test Security Guidebook:
Preventing, Detecting, and Investigating Test Security Irregularities.*
Washington, DC: Council of Chief State School Officers.

Copyright © 2013 by the Council of Chief State School Officers, Washington, DC
All rights reserved.

TABLE OF CONTENTS

Test security is a critical issue for many states and districts. Cheating and test piracy (stealing of test forms or items) pose major threats to the validity of test score interpretation and the credibility of large scale assessment programs. The soundness of test results requires systematic and productive efforts in all aspects of the design, development, and maintenance of these programs. States may need to make additional efforts to prevent cheating from occurring as well as detecting it if it has occurred. Currently, among the many issues that need to be addressed, some of the more crucial ones are those associated with the implementation of solid security procedures for high stakes assessments, at both the state and local levels. Not the least of these is the need to improve the professional testing practices of teachers.

Early in 2012, in response to recent attention across the country on improving the security of assessment programs, the Council of Chief State School Officers' Technical Issues in Large-Scale Assessment (TILSA) State Collaborative on Assessment and Student Standards launched a special project to assist states in proactively addressing potential security problems, including the development of this document, *Preventing, Detecting, and Investigating Test Security Irregularities: A Comprehensive Guidebook on Test Security for States*, hereafter referred to as the "guidebook." TILSA state members and experts on the topic collaborated on the contents of this guidebook to ensure the information provided is comprehensive in scope while remaining practical and useful to state assessment staff.

The main purpose of the guidebook is to provide resources that states can use for preventing and detecting irregularities, such as cheating and test piracy on state assessments, and for investigating suspected or confirmed instances of improper/unethical testing behavior by students or educators. The guidebook also provides depth on key technical topics such as data forensics analyses that state staff and others involved in testing will find it helpful in their ongoing work.

The guidebook focuses on three main test security issues: prevention, detection, and follow-up investigations. Discussion and details of security practices within the three topics include the following:

1. Prevention – Standards for the test security aspects of the design, development, and operation of state assessment programs, both paper and pencil and computer-based programs (with an emphasis on the latter), for both multiple choice response and performance measures.

2. Detection – Guidelines for planning, implementing, and interpreting data forensics analyses.

3. Follow-Up Investigations – Strategies for planning and conducting investigations and actions that states may need to take based on findings from investigations.

There are many recommendations throughout this guidebook. It seems reasonable, though, to list a limited number of critical recommendations for each of the three aspects of test security: prevention, detection, and follow-up investigation.

Prevention

- Devote as much attention as possible to prevention, even using announcements that you will be taking multiple steps to encourage adherence to testing rules and to discourage misbehavior. Include in your public outreach the consequences of failing to adhere to the rules of state testing.

- Assign responsibility for test security and monitor the effectiveness of the state's efforts.

- Limit testing windows to the extent feasible.

- Provide security training to all staff, both when they move into jobs and periodically to be sure they are current on security policies and procedures.

Detection

- Have your plans for employing data forensics reviewed and evaluated from a legal and a communications perspective.

- Employ data forensics analyses regularly for all high stakes programs. Use several different data forensics approaches, appropriate to the type of assessment program you are administering. The magnitude of score improvement will be a valuable indicator regardless of the type of program you have. Other analyses will depend on the program. For example, erasure analyses are recommended for paper and pencil examinations and analyses of time spent on items are recommended for computer-based tests.

- Develop interpretive guidelines for using data forensics analyses as a basis for action and include in staff training the interpretation and use of data forensics results.

Follow-Up Investigation

- Be conservative when interpreting and acting on data forensics results. Do not act on every statistically significant finding. Investigate and move on the "worst of the worst." Consider all in-depth investigations as efforts to clarify results, not attempts to prove people guilty.

- When a decision is made that the data forensics merit an in-depth investigation, always respect the privacy and professionalism of all individuals involved in the investigation.

- Maintain comprehensive records of any investigations in a form suitable for sharing in a court of law.

I. INTRODUCTION AND OVERVIEW

Background and Context on Test Security Issues in the Nation and States

Test security of state assessments has become an increasingly important topic as media across the nation buzz with stories of cheating in schools. As the stakes in state assessments increase, more instances of cheating by educators are being discovered. Increasingly, inappropriate practices have been emerging that have critical implications for very high stakes assessments. The implementation of mandatory use of student assessment results for teacher evaluation in the accountability systems of many states has increased the stakes even more. Effective test security is more crucial than ever to the maintenance of valid and reliable testing. State assessment programs need to be proactive about test security issues to promote confidence and ensure integrity in the overall testing program.

By late 2011, test security was one of the hottest topics and most critical of issues in many states and districts. The twin threats of cheating and test piracy to the credibility of testing programs and the soundness of test results require systematic efforts in the design, development, and maintenance of state assessment programs. One of the many issues that must be addressed is the implementation of solid security procedures for high stakes assessments — at both the state and local levels — and the need to improve the professional testing practices of teachers.

Also, in 2011 the work of the two Race to the Top (RTTT) assessment consortia began to have a major impact on states. Both the Partnership for Assessment of Readiness for College and Careers (PARCC) and the Smarter Balanced Assessment Consortium (SBAC) plan to use computer-based testing (CBT) as their main method of delivering the new assessments, as are other consortia that are developing alternate assessments and English language proficiency tests. However, there are many potential security threats and weak points to consider when using computer-based assessments, especially around the test administration process. Long testing windows are the most troublesome feature in a world where limited numbers of terminals and other devices are available in secure conditions. In places where CBT is being introduced, unfamiliarity with equipment and procedures will be widespread. The expression "a chain is only as strong as its weakest link" is highly relevant.

In January 2012, the U.S. Department of Education (USED) called for states to ensure the integrity of their assessment programs and the reported results. The practicalities of state departments of education (DOEs) being able to address the growing list of issues related to test security, especially in a time of limited resources, has created a "perfect storm" of conditions that need to be addressed quickly. Unfortunately, very few agencies have the breadth of expertise needed to take all the essential steps needed to respond with total confidence to the USED's call for the integrity of their assessment programs. Shifting to a new assessment delivery model such as computer delivered or even computer adaptive testing does not make cheating and test piracy problems go away. The problems merely take a different form. In Chapter III, security issues related to computer- and paper-based test administrations are addressed in more detail and a table of potential risks is provided.

TILSA Test Security Project

Because of all the attention being given to improving the security of assessment programs, TILSA created a new project to assist states in addressing their test security planning and strategies. The Test Security Project was initiated during the February 2012 meeting of TILSA, and John Olson and John Fremer were contracted as project directors and authors of this document, *Preventing, Detecting, and Investigating Test Security Irregularities: A Comprehensive Guidebook on Test Security for States*, hereafter referred to as the "guidebook." The authors have extensive experience in the prevention and detection of cheating on high stakes assessments. They have worked closely with many states in recent years to strengthen procedures to prevent testing irregularities and compromises of state assessment programs, and they have provided many practical and proven recommendations on how to improve test security at the state, district, and school levels.

A Test Security Workgroup — composed of state, associate, and affiliate members of TILSA — also was formed. The authors worked closely with the TILSA Workgroup to collaborate on the design of this guidebook and to solicit and receive input from states so that the content would be practical and useful to state assessment staff. Input from a variety of stakeholders, which included feedback from TILSA members, testing organizations, and experts on the topic of test security, has ensured the guidebook is comprehensive in scope.

An initial step in this project was to develop a survey on test security issues and collect data from all TILSA state members. The survey gathered information on existing policies and practices in states surrounding test security standards, audits, statistical analyses, investigations, and state issues and needs regarding test security. The data from the survey served as a needs assessment to help guide the direction of the project and the content of the guidebook.

For example, based on the results of this survey, more than 90 percent of the states that responded said that they have formal policies and procedures regarding cheating, train staff on test security procedures, and designate an individual responsible for test security investigations. However, all or most states also said they would like to get more information on guidelines for performing security audits; types of available data forensics approaches, and strengths and weaknesses of each; and potential roles for state level staff, school district staff, and possible outside agencies in an investigation. This guidebook addresses those issues.

In addition, throughout the course of the one-year project (2012-2013), monthly conference calls were held with the TILSA leadership to coordinate activities and review progress of the project. These regular meetings with TILSA's Leadership Team provided an opportunity to report on the progress of the project and to receive guidance and feedback. Topics discussed included the content and structure of the guidebook, strategies for obtaining and using information on state practices and needs for information, and other practical ideas.

Overview of the Comprehensive Guidebook on Test Security

The main purpose of this guidebook is to provide resources that states can use for preventing and detecting irregularities, such as cheating and test piracy, on state assessments and for investigating suspected or confirmed examples of improper or unethical testing behavior by either students or educators. It is written at a detailed level to provide depth on key technical topics such as data forensics analysis so that states' assessment staff and others involved in testing will find support and guidance for their ongoing work.

The guidebook focuses on three key aspects of test security: prevention, detection, and follow-up investigations.

1. Prevention – Standards for the test security aspects of the design, development, and operation of state assessment programs, both paper and pencil and computer-based programs (with an emphasis on the latter), for both multiple choice response and performance measures (see Chapter III).

2. Detection – Guidelines for planning, implementing, and interpreting data forensics analyses (see Chapter IV).

3. Follow-Up Investigations – Strategies for planning and conducting investigations and actions that states may need to take based on findings from investigations (see Chapter V).

Details on these three topics are provided in their respective chapters. Additionally the guidebook provides an overview, summary of recent/ongoing test security activities, a summary and recommendations, and appendices containing additional materials and resources for states. Important resources on the topic of test security are provided in the resources section and in the appendices, along with hyperlinks and website addresses for further information.

Please note the guidebook is organized so that each individual chapter can serve as a standalone resource for easy access by state assessment staff and others.

Use of the Guidebook by States and the Race to the Top (RTTT) Common Assessment Consortia

The information contained in the guidebook can be used by state staff and others who want to find out more about best practices regarding test security and/or are thinking about improving their policies and procedures for their state assessment program.

A key issue for a consortium of states, related to the establishment of a test window, is how to ensure the security of the assessment measures used, especially in the present day world of the Internet where news (and test items) can spread across the country in minutes. States participating in a consortium will need to think carefully about maintaining test security and thus preserving the validity of test score interpretations. The consortium must collectively determine how long the assessment window will be open for each content area and grade level. States with limited computer resources will need to have longer test windows. This will have to be balanced with the understanding that the longer a test window is open, the more likely the assessment materials will be compromised. A possible solution might be for the consortium to develop multiple forms of the assessment to be used, and develop an administration plan to offer or distribute the multiple forms. Whereas there are technical and cost implications for this recommendation, this strategy would enhance test security. For example, students in some states might take the same test form if testing is done on the same days, but use different forms if the test is administered on different days (or weeks). Another approach is to use a computer adaptive testing (CAT) model, where the computer essentially creates multiple forms and administers a different one to each student.

For states in a consortium, neither online administration nor CAT can completely assure test security. Students who are not monitored closely can copy down or take photos of test questions during or following testing and then share them widely on social media such as Facebook and Twitter. It will matter little whether students were tested on paper or online.

A consortium will need to carefully consider its policies and determine how to protect its assessment items and instruments. The solution may well be a combination of a large bank of items for use online and multiple paper-based forms to use both within and across states. In addition, policies for the distribution and administration of tests and the length of the testing windows also will have a bearing on the solution to this dilemma.

There are many practical documents and resources included in various parts of the guidebook. For example, sample checklists to improve test security prevention processes for each phase of an assessment are included; an example outline of a test security manual is presented; and a model investigations kit with sample interview guides, forms, timelines, and suggested allocation of responsibilities is provided.

A crucial area where the guidebook can be applied within states is with the promotion of professional best practice for school administrators and teachers. An important objective of this project is to guide educators on appropriate ways to conduct testing in their schools, with the hope of improving the procedures being used and the overall validity and fairness of the assessment results.

Finally, readers should note the guidebook is intended to be accessible to a wide audience which may include — but is not limited to — assessment personnel, psychometricians, and testing organizations. Although the guidebook mainly focuses on addressing issues that pertain to state and district assessment staff such as assessment directors who will be most responsible for implementing the recommendations provided, others may be interested in the information as well. This includes many other staff in state education agencies (SEAs) and local school districts, as well as state leadership, policymakers at the state and local levels, reporters, and other key stakeholders. Thus, as much as possible, given the nature and content of the report, it has been written in a non-technical, yet practical and applicable manner.

II. ONGOING/RECENT ACTIVITIES RELATED TO TEST SECURITY FOR NATIONAL AND STATE ASSESSMENTS

This chapter provides a brief summary of some ongoing and recent activities related to test security. In the past year (2011-2012), many new activities have occurred that are influencing the directions states are headed in addressing issues and concerns for the security of their assessment programs. The intent here is to highlight some of the most critical national and state activities and give the reader information on how to get more details if desired. Wherever possible, hyperlinks to websites are provided for further information and to help readers obtain the most up-to-date materials available.

In addition, members of Technical Issues in Large-Scale Assessment (TILSA) have member-level access to the CCSSO Spaces website (spaces.ccsso.org) where various documents and materials on test security have been placed.

U.S. Department of Education Request for Information on Testing Integrity. In January 2012, the U.S. Department of Education (USED) issued a request for information (RFI) to collect information from experts and others on test security issues. The following was stated in the official notice:

> *"In light of recent, high-profile reports of misconduct by school officials in the test administration process, the U.S. Department of Education ("the Department" or "we") is seeking to collect and share information about best practices that have been used to prevent, detect, and respond to irregularities in academic testing. To that end, the Department is taking several steps, described below, to collect information and gather suggestions to assist State educational agencies (SEAs), local educational agencies (LEAs), and the testing-integrity-focused organizations that service them. The Department anticipates making use of this information to facilitate further dialogue and to help SEAs and LEAs identify, share, and implement best practices for preventing, detecting, and investigating irregularities in academic testing.*
>
> *First, the Department is issuing this request for information (RFI) to collect information about the integrity of academic testing. We pose a series of questions to which we invite interested members of the public to respond. Second, the Department will host a symposium where external experts can engage in further discussion and probe these issues in greater depth. Third, the Department will publish a document that contains a summary of the recommendations that were developed as a result of the RFI and the symposium, as well as other resources identified by external experts participating in the symposium."*

A summary of the information obtained through the USED RFI was issued in February 2013, entitled "Issues and Recommendations for Best Practice." The report is available at

http://nces.ed.gov/pubsearch/pubsinfo.asp?pubid=2013454.

National Center for Education Statistics Special Symposium on Test Integrity. In February 2012, USED implemented the second step from their RFI as noted above. The National Center for Education Statistics (NCES) hosted a testing integrity symposium to examine important issues in academic testing, and a distinguished body of expert panelists shared best practices for

- Prevention of testing irregularities;
- Detection and analysis of testing irregularities;
- Response and investigation of alleged testing irregularities; and
- Discussion of testing integrity practices and procedures for online and computer-based assessments.

Four panels of experts were recruited to address a wide spectrum of issues on test security and shared useful information. The presentation materials, a webcast, and a transcript of proceedings from the symposium is available at

http://ies.ed.gov/whatsnew/conferences/?id=966 .

Data Forensics Summit at University of Kansas. In May 2012, the Center for Educational Testing and Evaluation (CETE) at the University of Kansas in collaboration with a number of other testing organizations held a conference on Statistical Detection of Potential Test Fraud. This was the first scholarly conference focusing on statistical approaches to identifying test fraud, a growing concern as methods of test administration evolve and new ways of committing test fraud emerge. The conference provided researchers the opportunity to learn about, share, and discuss those statistical methods that testing organizations have developed and used over the years to look for test fraud. It was a forum for scholars and those working in the testing field to examine with their colleagues a variety of methods to counter test fraud. **Topics at the conference sessions included** answer-changing behaviors (including erasure analysis), macro-level cheating in schools, similarities in test responses, detection of aberrant responses, statistical methods to detect test fraud, and test security.

More information on the conference and the papers that were shared can be found at

http://www.cete.us/conference2012/ .

CCSSO/Association of Test Publishers *Operational Best Practices for Statewide Large-Scale Assessment Programs (2010).* In 2006, the Association of Test Publishers (ATP) and CCSSO began work to identify and publish a set of voluntary, non-regulatory best practices for states and testing companies to use to strengthen implementation of statewide testing programs under the No Child Left Behind Act (NCLB). *Operational Best Practices for Statewide Large-Scale Assessment Programs* was published in 2010 and an updated version is in progress. ATP and CCSSO believe that this document provides a solid framework from which others might seek to define a set of practices tailored to their testing programs; accordingly, ATP and CCSSO encourage others to use this document for that purpose. Moreover, the two organizations fully recognize that the testing process is not static; therefore, the publication will be reviewed on a periodic basis and updated to account for changes in technology or testing methodologies (e.g., a growing reliance on online testing), to ensure that content remains viable.

In 2011, ATP and CCSSO worked with state assessment directors to include a new chapter on test security in the book. This new chapter is intended to be a companion document reflective of the practical and useful text found in the test security chapter of the first edition of the book. As of late-2012, the chapter on test security had been drafted and was being reviewed for inclusion in the second edition of this important document. For more information on the current and forthcoming versions of the "Operational Best Practices" documents, see http://www.ccsso.org/resources/publications/operational_best_practices_for_statewide_large-scale_assessment_programs.html.

Association of Test Publishers (ATP) Security Council and Recent Meeting. The ATP Security Council was formed to advise membership on test security, specifically the detection and prevention of cheating. ATP held a conference in early 2012 and many of the highly-attended sessions dealt with topics related to test security. Session presentations focused on cheating on commercially available tests and high-stakes exams, and the increased attention on test security investigations for state and district assessments was a hot topic.

More information on ATP can be found at http://www.testpublishers.org.

National Council on Measurement in Education White Paper on Test Integrity. In 2012, Gregory Cizek, President of the National Council on Measurement in Education (NCME), led an initiative to address the issue of test integrity. A Test Score Integrity Work Group was formed and a set of best practices was developed. These best practices were documented in *Testing and Data Integrity in the Administration of Statewide Student Assessment Programs* (NCME, 2012), a paper which emphasizes that valid testing requires the results to be useful, interpretable, accurate, and comparable. The technical merits of the test scores must meet industry standards with respect to fairness, reliability, and validity; however, cheating and security breaches can pollute the data, reducing or eliminating their value. Comparability across states participating in a common assessment consortium could be jeopardized by cheating. When cheating occurs, the public loses confidence in the testing program and, by extension, in the educational system. Serious educational, fiscal, and political consequences can follow. The document suggests more efforts are needed to ensure test data integrity through policies and procedures that ensure all students have had equal opportunities to show their knowledge, skills, and abilities.

The paper provides a series of recommended practices for state and district entities. A cover letter from Cizek and a copy of the paper are provided in Appendix G.

Summary of TILSA Survey of State Members on Test Security Issues. As part of the work for this test security project, a survey of the TILSA states was conducted in April 2012 to gather information from members on a variety of issues related to test security. For the information gathering process, a survey was sent to all TILSA state members to learn about their current practices, challenges, and needs. Information from this survey was used to inform work on the project. The results of the survey are presented in four sections:

Section A: State Test Security Policies and Practices

Section B: State Test Security Breaches

Section C: What is Important/Worrisome to States?

Section D: What Information Should be in the TILSA Test Security Guidebook?

A complete copy of the results is provided in Appendix I.

State- and District-Level Academic Dishonesty Policies. In April 2012, CCSSO released a new report in which Hanover Research presented an overview of state- and district-level policies regarding academic dishonesty. The report reviews cheating policies established by educational bodies at the state and district levels across the U.S. Key findings and detailed information on specific state and district policies are summarized. A copy of the report's Introduction is provided in Appendix H. The full report may be requested by contacting Dr. John Olson at jmclkolson@ yahoo.com.

International Test Commission Guidelines on Test Security. During 2011 and 2012, testing experts from several countries worked on a set of test security guidelines. The International Test Commission (ITC) currently is working on publishing those guidelines. For more information on ITC and its future publications, please visit http://www.intestcom.org/guidelines.

Other Useful Documents and Information from States. During the course of the project, TILSA workgroup members provided various documents and other information from their assessment programs that could be useful to states. As noted earlier, these materials have been placed on the TILSA Spaces website for test security information.

In addition, Caveon Test Security, a specialized provider of test security services dedicated to detecting, correcting, and preventing test fraud, holds monthly webinars on a variety of test security issues, such as preventing online cheating on tests, conducting security investigations, and advice on how not to end up on the front page of local or national news publications. More information on these webinars can be found at http://www.caveon.com.

III. PREVENTION

This chapter addresses the challenge of preventing cheating on tests and compromises of test content, often described as "test piracy." The following areas are covered:

A. Paper and Pencil and Computer-Based Testing

B. Resources for Test Security Standards for Developing and Implementing State Assessment Programs

C. Test Security Checklists for Each Phase of Assessment

D. Staffing and Training

E. The Role of Security Audits

F. Additional Resources for States

A. Paper and Pencil and Computer-Based Testing

The need to protect the security of test questions and to prevent or detect cheating persists as states move to computer-based testing (CBT). Some problems either go away or change form when paper and pencil testing (P&P) is discontinued. Unless printed copies of test banks or test forms are created as part of the development process, it is not necessary, for example, to find a locked cabinet or room with supervision to protect test books throughout a testing period. The specter of an educator or other adult changing student answer sheets after the close of testing or filling out answer sheets for them is no longer a concern. It is still essential, however, to make sure to the extent feasible that students work independently during testing. We are interested in what the student knows and can do, not in the responses they would give with unauthorized assistance; thus, training for test administrators in proctoring responsibilities and monitoring of the testing process continues to be important. Whenever there are significant stakes associated with testing, there will be pressures to break the rules at both the test taker and test administrator levels.

Whether P&P or CBT administration is employed, it is also desirable to monitor the Internet for pirated assessment items. The introduction of the computer-based Race to the Top (RTTT) consortium assessments with long test administration windows makes this issue even more salient. Use of a computer adaptive testing (CAT) model with large item pools helps to significantly minimize the risks associated with prior exposure to test items, but leaves security vulnerabilities associated with providing improper assistance during testing or failing to ensure that students work on their own.

The following table outlines the types of security breaches that may occur for P&P, CBTs, or CATs. Asterisks show the potential risk to state assessment programs. Please note that the determination of the risk of a test security breach is somewhat subjective since the overall level of security risk depends on numerous factors, such as test design, item types, item exposure, quality of proctoring, the testing environment, conflicts of interest, methods for transmission and storage, encryption levels, quality of training, and more.

RISK OF VARIOUS TYPES OF TEST SECURITY BREACHES

BEFORE, DURING, AND AFTER	P&P	CBT	CAT
Lost or stolen booklets	*		
Obtaining unauthorized access to secure exam materials	*	*	*
Educators logging into tests to view questions or change responses		*	*
Hacking into computers		*	*
BEFORE			
Educators or students engaging others to take an exam on a student's behalf	*	*	*
DURING			
Students giving or receiving unauthorized assistance from other students during an examination	*	*	*
Teachers providing answers to students during testing	*	*	*
Students accessing non-allowable resources (notes, textbooks, the Internet)	*	*	*
Use of actual exam questions or answers during the test	*	*	*
Accommodations being used inappropriately to cheat	*	*	*
Keystroke logging		*	*
AFTER			
Altering exam scores	*	*	*
Reconstructing exam materials through memorization	*	*	*
Memorized test items or answers being posted online	*	*	*
Printing, emailing, or storing test information in a computer outside the test delivery system		*	*
Accessing test materials or scores during the transfer of data	*	*	*

B. Resources for Test Security Standards for the Development and Implementation of State Assessment Programs

Standards for test security have a fairly long history and state assessment staff may want to review some of the more noteworthy efforts. This section provides an overview of some of the documents that either may already be in the possession of state staff or warrant acquisition.

AERA/APA/NCME *Standards for Educational and Psychological Testing (1999)*

These standards are so fundamental to developing and managing testing programs that they are often simply referred to as "the standards." The current version was released in 1999, but a revision effort was underway as of the publication of this guidebook and is expected to be available by October 2013. The 1999 version has only six standards related to test security, but they cover key aspects:

- 5.6 – "...eliminate opportunities for test takers to attain scores by fraudulent means."
- 5.7 – "Test users have the responsibility of protecting the security of test materials at all times."
- 11.7 – [Same as 5.7]
- 11.11 – "If the integrity of a test taker's score is challenged...inform test takers of their relevant rights ..."
- 12.11 – "...ensure the confidentiality of test results..."
- 13.11 – "Ensure that any test preparation materials and activities...will not affect the validity of test score inferences."

Accreditation program for personnel certification bodies under ANSI/ISO/IEC 17024

Internationally recognized standards from the American National Standards Institute set forth requirements in many areas, including test security, which a certifying testing entity must meet. These standards were not designed for state assessment programs, but they not only have specific standards that apply to virtually all high stakes programs, they are embedded in a review process worth evaluating and imitating, including conducting security audits, a process described later in this chapter.

Caveon Test Security Standards (2003 and subsequent years)

The Caveon Test Security Standards contain much more detail than is ordinarily present in testing standards as they were designed to support a comprehensive test security audit of 15 areas related to the design, development, and operation of a testing program. The Caveon standards are included in Appendix C.

CCSSO/ATP *Operational Best Practices for Statewide Large-Scale Assessment Programs (2010)*

In 2006, the Association of Test Publishers (ATP) and CCSSO began discussions to identify and publish a set of voluntary, non-regulatory best practices for states and testing companies to use to strengthen implementation of statewide testing programs under the No Child Left Behind Act (NCLB). The idea for developing a best practices document originated with the U.S. Department of Education (USED). This concept reflected a belief that such a document would facilitate quality testing practices for the benefit of everyone affected by state testing programs, including schools, parents, and students. *Operational Best Practices for Statewide Large-Scale Assessment Programs* was published in 2010 and an updated version based on CBT is in progress.

To best develop state-specific security standards, each state needs an overall strategy goal related to ultimately providing fair and valid test results. Additionally, as outlined in the current version of *Operational Best Practices for Statewide Large-Scale Assessment Programs*, adopted security standards should cover these areas:

- Program Management
- Test Design and Deployment
- Scoring and Reporting
- Quality Control

Each of these areas is further described below based on the ATP/CCSSO publication, found at

http://www.ccsso.org/resources/publications/operational_best_practices_for_statewide_large-scale_assessment_programs.html.

Program Management

1. Security Plan – A formal, written document covering internal processes such as item development; field/pilot testing; test construction; materials production and distribution; scoring; data processing and analyses; and reporting. The plan should cover goals, policies and procedures, definitions, staff roles and responsibilities, and approvals.

2. Budget and Funding – The budget and contingency funding for security purposes.

3. Protection of Intellectual Property – A comprehensive plan to protect the security of intellectual property of paper and electronic data and materials, including items and test pools.

4. Staffing – Procedures should be established and implemented to handle selection and responsibilities of all personnel who have access to secure materials.

Test Design and Deployment

5. Test and Item Design (including the use of item types and test designs that promote test security) – Although the primary consideration in test and item development should be alignment to the purposes and constructs that a test is designed to address, tests and items should be also designed, as much as possible, for security purposes. The design should discourage memorization and sharing, and make common methods of cheating less effective. Test and item designs should limit item exposure, thereby prolonging the usefulness of items and test results.

6. Test/Item Development and Maintenance – Procedures and rules should be established and implemented to secure items, item pools, and associated data during periods of item and test development.

7. Test Publication – After the test has been created, it is published and distributed. Security measures must be in place to protect it during this period. These measures need to address security of electronic files, especially banks of test items and test forms as well as print copies of secure test materials whether for P&P or computer-delivered tests.

Test Administration and Scoring

8. Test Administration – Procedures and rules should be developed, implemented, and communicated to all interested parties to keep tests secure before, during, and after test administration. Test administration refers to the process of registering examinees, scheduling, providing physical security measures, presenting the test content, gathering the test results, and delivering and communicating results and other information to the organization.

9. Test Scores and Results – Procedures and rules should be established and implemented to assure appropriate scoring with no irregularities and correcting student responses. In addition, procedures should be established for detecting irregularities in student test scores.

Quality Control

10. Physical Security – Tests, and the systems and materials needed to develop tests, must be secure in a testing program's facilities during every phase of the test development and production process.

11. Information Security – Digital and physical information related to the organization's testing program must be stored and transmitted securely at all times.

12. Web and Media Monitoring (checking the Internet for test content) – With the Internet's ubiquity, it is critical that a high-stakes testing program monitor for the disclosure of its copyrighted items and other test information. It is not sufficient to simply have a process for detecting secure content on the web — it is also essential to have a plan and program for getting material taken down as quickly as possible and to deter future posting of test items or comments about test items that compromise their security.

13. Security Awareness and Training – The program should take proper steps to place the value of a security plan and specific security problems into perspective, and to disclose and use security information carefully. For example, asking all who administer tests to confirm that they have received training in the state's assessment procedures and will adhere to (or have adhered) these standards is a desirable security practice. It is also helpful to remind students at the time of testing that they are to respond to questions on their own without any assistance and that it is not permissible to communicate about the specifics of test content after they have taken the tests.

C. Test Security Checklists for Each Phase of Assessment

In addition to developing a set of state standards for test security, it is useful for states to have one or more corresponding checklists of key steps that would help to monitor the security conditions within key phases of state assessment program development and management. In this section checklists are presented for the following areas:

1. Program Management

2. Test Publication or Deployment

3. Test Administration and Scoring

4. Quality Control

Each state will likely need to customize these checklists for the specific circumstances of each state and testing program, including the resources available for test program development, operation, and management. The goal of each program should be to maintain a high level of test security. The particular strategies employed to accomplish that result will vary from state to state so the checklist that will guide the development and management of a state assessment program will reflect judgments of the assessment program managers and the circumstances within which assessment occurs (e.g., P&P versus CBT and how the results are used).

1. Program Management

✓ Adopt security standards that include the use of data forensics analyses (the use of analytic methods to identify or detect possible cheating) as a basic component of test scoring and test analyses

✓ Emphasize and reinforce the importance of test security

✓ Assign responsibility for test security

✓ Include use of data forensics analyses in requests for proposals (RFPs) and vendor contracts (see Appendix E for sample language)

✓ Obtain and maintain non-disclosure agreements from all who touch state assessments

✓ Provide and update security training on data forensics use to state assessment staff

✓ Obtain legal reviews of plans to use data forensics results

2. Test Publication or Deployment

✓ Learn about the data forensics approaches supported by testing vendors

✓ Limit testing windows to the extent feasible

- ✓ Employ record keeping strategies for testing events that will facilitate follow-up investigations suggested by data forensics results

- ✓ Include in administration manuals and other information materials the fact that the assessment program will be performing data forensics analyses

- ✓ Include data forensics explanations with examples in district and school test coordinator training

- ✓ Prepare assessment staff for use of data forensics results using vendor assistance for this purpose

- ✓ Provide a help line for school staff to ask questions about the use of data forensics methods

3. Scoring and Reporting

- ✓ Develop a plan for using data forensics results before analyzing the test data

- ✓ Obtain legal and communications review of the plan

- ✓ Assign responsibility for managing the follow-up actions that will be based on the data forensics findings

- ✓ Employ a variety of data forensics methods

- ✓ Include gain scores, analyses directed at detecting inappropriate collaboration among test takers, and examinee model misfit analyses in all data forensics approaches regardless of test delivery method

- ✓ Include erasure analyses for P&P, but do not rely only on this approach

- ✓ Include response latency and other test taking time analyses in CBT

- ✓ Investigate the most significant, from a practical perspective, data forensics results

- ✓ Take any necessary steps to permit use of data forensics results as the sole evidence to invalidate scores or take other actions

- ✓ Follow through thoroughly on all clear evidence of testing irregularities

- ✓ Keep good records of the handing and disposition of data forensics cases

- ✓ Review the data forensics results regularly to evaluate the impact of the results on the number of testing irregularities

4. Quality Control

- ✓ Assign responsibility for physical security for test materials to an assessment staff member

- ✓ Ensure that all test and other confidential materials are kept and transmitted under secure conditions

✓ Collect and destroy all test materials created during the development process that are no longer needed

✓ Protect the confidentiality of personal information at all stages of testing and reporting

✓ Archive and back up all critical test material in a secure way

✓ Monitor the Internet periodically for secure test material and other information

✓ Periodically review the effectiveness of monitoring procedures and outcomes

✓ Provide security training to all staff, both when they move into jobs and periodically to be sure that staff are current on policies and procedures as well as aware of threats to the test materials

D. Staffing and Training

State assessment programs have well established and widely used methods of training the teachers and administrators responsible for testing in schools and other sites. Each district usually has a district test coordinator who receives training, typically annually, at workshops planned and conducted by state assessment staff or a testing vendor often with the participation of both entities. The district test coordinator, in turn, is responsible for training school test coordinators who then must train those that administer the state tests, typically teachers in the schools. Sometimes webinars or other Internet-based training is employed to deliver training.

Although security training is a part of what district and school test coordinators receive, the amount of attention devoted to security is often quite limited especially with respect to cheating analyses, and district test coordinators often do not receive special PowerPoint slides or other materials that they can use when doing their training for school staff. The group receiving training may also not be closely tracked and recorded so that only trained individuals administer exams. Rules for who should administer or monitor test administrations may also not be very specific. Such lack of specificity can lead to a great deal of variation in who is involved in test administration from school to school.

The issue of security training related to data forensics analyses merits sustained attention by state assessment and vendor staff. As a start, the assessment staff at the state department should have their own training program, one that is comprehensive and regularly updated. The task of defining and delivering content on data forensics needs to be a staff member's ongoing responsibility. Materials that are developed or acquired from a vendor, another state, or an organization such as the Technical Issues in Large-Scale Assessment (TILSA) state collaborative should get legal reviews as well as reviews by the communications staff. State assessment staff should ask

• What messages are we sending with our training materials?

• Are those messages fully consistent with our security goals?

- Do we make it very clear without sounding like "big brother" that we expect all rules to be followed by teachers and administrators?

- Do materials specify who is to have access to test materials or testing rooms and under what circumstances?

- Is it clear that the roles of test proctors have been clearly and explicitly conveyed?

- Is there a "duty to report" problems or to intervene to correct problematic situations?

- Does everyone know that there will be unannounced monitoring of testing by state level staff or other authorized observers?

- Does everyone know the use that the state will be making of data forensics analyses and what their responsibilities might be?

In the U.S., occasions of misbehavior by educators in state assessments are relatively rare compared to other types of testing programs and to educational testing in other countries. To maintain this situation requires conscientious planning, delivery, and monitoring. A major part of the challenge for state assessment staff is that the security situation with students is far worse than that for educators. Student cheating has been rising consistently for decades and is more prevalent the older the student, so there is more cheating in the upper grades than in the lower ones, and that pattern continues into the college years. (See, for example a review of some of Donald McCabe's extensive research on cheating in Vega, 2012.)

It is the case that students have thoroughly incorporated communications technologies into their everyday lives. Many students can send and receive messages without even glancing at their cell phone or other device. So a student may appear to be intently focused on a computer screen or test booklet and at the same time be engaging in testing misbehavior. For security purposes, forbidding cell phones at the student's desk is the best administration strategy. Many methods of handling this situation have been developed, including having a cell phone basket in the front of the testing room or having students place their cell phones in a clear plastic bag that hangs behind their seat. Enforcing a "no cell phone at testing time" policy requires conscientious effort. It is of little value for a student to surrender one cell phone when they still have another that is concealed. It is essential to communicate zero tolerance for retaining a cell phone in the testing environment. Test administrators need to receive training in the state's rules regarding cell phones, on what to look for at the time of testing, and in what to do if misbehavior is suspected or detected.

E. The Role of Security Audits

To make sure that all components of the security of an assessment program are being planned and managed in a systematic and effective way, they should be evaluated by a thorough audit of all aspects of the design, development, and operation of a state assessment program. To be most valuable, the test security audit should have the following features:

- Be conducted by expert staff from outside the state assessment program or its test development and delivery vendors;

- Be conducted by staff with firsthand knowledge of state testing policies and practices;

- Be guided by formal test security standards; and

- Result in the identification of security vulnerabilities as well as recommendations for dealing with these vulnerabilities.

The rationale for each of these recommendations follows:

Use of Non-Program Testing Professionals

It is very appropriate for the staff who develop and administer testing programs to periodically review the security features of their program, including policies, procedures, and materials. However, the creators of a state assessment program are not the best in-depth evaluators of the security features of that program, especially the identification of areas needing improvement. It is like asking parents to evaluate their own children. Parents will eagerly tell you how talented, bright, and personally appealing their children are. This is very fine set of attitudes for a parent to have, but since most parents will say the same thing about their children, you don't get very good information about skills and competencies, or areas of possible weakness. Teachers and other knowledgeable observers can provide a more objective perspective.

Similarly, state assessment staff should use outside objective and knowledgeable professionals to evaluate the security aspects of testing programs. This type of outside look is very common in financial matters and occurs also with the information technology (IT) aspects of most high-stakes testing programs, including state assessments. Many of the features of financial and IT security audits need to be applied to test security audits in order to get the maximum benefit from the security audit process.

Using Auditors Who Know State Testing

There are many distinctive features of state assessment programs that need to be known by security auditors for their work to be of maximum value to a state. The specifics of each state also need to be learned by the auditors. It should not be necessary, though, to explain the basic mechanisms such as the use of district and school test coordinators, the use of classroom teachers as the primary test administrators, and the need to clearly distinguish among various types of test preparation. Test security auditors need to know that some forms of test preparation are clearly appropriate (e.g., explaining the rules of testing and providing access to sample tests) and that others are clearly inappropriate (e.g., presenting actual operational items). That class of information needs to be known by auditors before they begin their audits.

Use Formal Test Security Standards

As is the case with financial and IT audits, formal test security standards should be the basis for the test security audits. Fortunately over the past few years such standards have become much more widely available. The initial discussion in this chapter draws on the CCSSO/ATP (2010) operational best practices standards. It is also useful to review the standards for the certification of testing programs used by the American National Standards Institute (see http://www.ansi.org). Standards from Caveon Test Security are included in this guidebook (Appendix C), and the test security chapters in the *Operational Best Practices for Statewide Large-Scale Assessment Programs* (CCSSO/ATP, 2010) — both the current and draft versions — contain information on CBT which can be valuable to security auditors.

Identifying Security Vulnerabilities and Recommending Remedies

The outcome of a test security audit should not only be the identification of security vulnerabilities, but also the presentation of specific and practical remedies for these vulnerabilities. All state assessment programs that carry high stakes, be they P&P or CBT, have security vulnerabilities. To minimize test security threats, state assessment staff need to learn where their program is vulnerable and how these vulnerabilities can be addressed. The vulnerabilities most often noted in test security audits at the state level are

- Processes often need documentation and a method to confirm that the reader is looking at the most recent version.

- There are often few training materials for state assessment staff.

- Management of cell phones and other communication devices at testing sites is often inconsistent.

- Help is frequently needed in interpreting statistical results to determine the need for action.

Once security vulnerabilities have been identified, assessment staff can then develop plans and schedules consistent with the life cycles of their programs and available staff and resources.

It is fairly common for state assessment staff to cite budget constraints as barriers to upgrading test security for state assessments. States have already made a significant investment in these tests. They cost multiple millions of dollars to develop so it is not unreasonable to devote some money to protecting their integrity. Attending to test security concerns, however, should not be viewed as an optional component of a program. Unless security is maintained, the fairness and validity of state tests becomes suspect. Quite frankly, state assessment staff can't afford *not* to address test security issues. They are a critical part of a well-managed program that produces results that are a worthy basis for actions and evaluations.

One of the issues for the state assessment consortia is the placement of security procedures and analyses. What will be done across states and what is reserved for individual states to manage? This is a very important issue as the staffing and procedures necessary to monitor the security of test materials need to be planned, piloted, and implemented in accordance with the kinds of policies and procedures covered in this guidebook and other cited and referenced documents.

F. Additional Resources for States

Chapter II outlined a number of projects that are useful references for states. In this section, the guidebook discusses where states can go for additional information and assistance with the challenge of maintaining item security and test program information, while also preventing cheating. Citations and/or website addresses for the items listed below were provided in Chapter II and are not repeated here. (Note: A comprehensive list of resources is provided in the Resources section of this guidebook.)

Professional Library

- Although somewhat dated, the book *Cheating on Tests* (Cizek, 1999) should be in all state assessment units. The book provides a good primer on how cheating on tests takes place, and how it can be detected and prevented.

- Interested parties can access the PowerPoint slides from the February 2012 NCES Testing Integrity Symposium. There were many insightful observations about dealing with potential cheating from the academic community, state and district staff, and the assessment profession and industry. See the Resources section for details on how to access this information.

- *Handbook of Test Security* (Wollack & Fremer, forthcoming) is the newest work on test security and will be available March 2013. The book has 17 chapters covering many test security issues that will be of interest to state assessment staff.

Testing Vendors

The issue of maintaining the security of items and tests is shared by the test vendor community. If states make it clear in RFPs (see the sample language in Appendix E) and in regular meetings with vendors that they are expecting excellent assistance in attaining and maintaining security, vendors will want to meet or exceed the security requirements. One challenge that state staff share with testing vendor staff is that there was relatively little attention given to detecting cheating in the psychometric graduate programs that trained most senior staff. Even now a good deal of what is known is the result of "on the job" learning as staff worked hard to understand and deal with problems as they came up.

Professional Conferences

Traditionally, the CCSSO National Conference on Student Assessment (NCSA) has been a very good source of papers and discussions of "hot issues" such as test security. It is strongly recommended that individual states make their interests and concerns regarding test security very clear to NCSA staff and the program planning committee early in the planning phase of future conferences.

ATP's conference is another where test security receives a great deal of attention. Its focus is broader than state assessments, but ATP has collaborated with CCSSO to produce the *Operational Best Practices for Statewide Large-Scale Assessment Programs* (2010) publication discussed earlier. For states that are in a position to have a staff member at more than one testing conference in a year, the ATP conference is well worth considering.

For state staff interested in the statistical detection of cheating, 2012 was the year and the University of Kansas the location of the first conference devoted exclusively to that topic. States should obtain the slides from that meeting (see Chapter II) and consider attending follow-up conferences such as the one scheduled for the University of Wisconsin in October 2013.

IV. DETECTION

The detection of cheating and piracy of test questions on state assessments is addressed in this chapter. The following areas are covered:

A. Types of Data Forensics Methods and their Strengths and Weaknesses

B. Preparing Local Education Agencies for the Use of Data Forensics Information

C. Legal and Regulatory Issues Regarding the Use of Data Forensics in State Assessments

A. Types of Data Forensics Methods and their Strengths and Weaknesses

Data forensics for state tests is the use of analytic methods to identify or detect possible cheating. Data forensics methods are used in many areas. In medicine, for example, data forensics track the course of illnesses and the effectiveness and cost of particular treatments. They are also used in sales and marketing studies to evaluate the effectiveness of sales and marketing campaigns. Data forensics is also used extensively in law enforcement to evaluate bodies of evidence as related to a possible crime.

Data forensics methods are valuable in the detection of cheating regardless of whether a test is administered via paper and pencil or by computer. Many of the analyses are very similar regardless of the delivery approach (e.g., comparison of scores across two occasions or the consistency of a test taker's responses across questions of varying levels of difficulty). Other analyses vary by the type of delivery. The analyses of erasures done for paper and pencil tests (P&P) rely on the interpretation of answer sheet marks of different degrees of darkness with light marks meeting certain criteria being interpreted as erasures. In a computer administered testing environment, the sequence of responses is typically recorded by the testing system so it is possible to compare first and second or later responses. Computer based testing (CBT) also permits detailed analyses of the response times of test takers (latency analysis). On occasion, test takers will proceed through a test answering all questions correctly and using less time than it would take almost any test taker to even read the questions, let alone choose the answers. These test takers have very different response times from most other test takers. In some instances, test takers may well be "harvesting" test questions to facilitate cheating at a later time.

In both CBT and P&P settings, very similar questions need to be asked, but the particular methods for answering the questions vary somewhat with the format. Here are the kinds of questions that data forensics methods can help answer:

- Does it appear that two or more test takers colluded before or during a test?

- Does it appear that some students had advance knowledge of specific test questions?

- Is there evidence that the responses of two or more students in a class are far more similar than would have occurred if they were working independently?

- In CBT, is the timing of responses to questions extremely different from how other students allocated their time?

- Are there changes in test scores for an individual or a class from one test administration to another that are much greater than one would expect for the test that was administered?

The following sections of this chapter look at the data forensics methods most frequently employed by states and the strengths and weaknesses of each approach as well as any differences in approach for P&P and computer-delivered tests.

Data Forensics Overview Table

As an advance organizer for the discussion of data forensics methods, the following table lists the methods discussed and the types of testing irregularities they help detect:

DATA FORENSICS ANALYSIS	TESTING IRREGULARITIES
Unusual Score Gains or Losses	Coaching on actual test content, "helping" during an examination
Similarity Analyses	Sharing answers during testing, teachers helping before or during testing, illicit use of stolen test questions
Erasure (Answer Changing) Analyses	Changing answers by educators, inappropriate assistance during testing
Person Fit Analyses	Inconsistent response patterns such as answering difficult questions correctly while missing easy questions
Other Data Forensics Methods (e.g., response time analyses)	Varies

Unusual Score Gains and Losses

The data forensics approach that is easiest to employ and which has a very long history of use in state assessments is making comparisons of scores from one testing occasion to another. As noted, this approach is essentially the same regardless of the test delivery method. The data needed to perform such analyses are provided by testing vendors to states and are often available on the websites of individual school districts. Because it is relatively easy to obtain the data to compare scores over time, many media stories about possible cheating use this information. When employing score comparisons as a method of making judgments about whether inappropriate behavior may have occurred, it is important to keep in mind that the goal of school staff is that of helping their students learn as much of the content of the state's curriculum as is feasible. So, all across a state, educators are attempting to bring about improvement in student performance, and increasingly being held accountable for that very improvement. School staffs can be very skeptical of challenges to their testing practices, particularly when the results are high. They may view those higher results as being solely the result of students achieving higher levels of learning through improved instruction as opposed to a possible security breach.

It is essential that the score comparisons make proper use of the data that are available. Where many comparisons are being made, such as looking at all the results at a particular grade level across all subjects for every school, there will be some substantial differences even when all rules were followed scrupulously. Schools need to involve statistical and psychometric staff in analyses they perform or as part of their own review of analyses done by others such as news media staff and consultants.

In carrying out score gain and loss analyses, states and schools will find the results most useful if data are analyzed over several years. Generally year to year changes for large groups will be relatively small and consistent with the educational activities at the school and any changes in the composition of the student groups and educational programs that the test results reflect. Reports should be clear also as to what is being compared. Are data users looking at the results for this year's fourth graders, for example, and comparing them with the performance of last year's fourth graders? Sometimes schools follow students up to the next level and compare this year's fifth graders with last year's fourth graders. In that approach, it is important to recognize that in mathematics, for example, course objectives vary from year to year so while one can make judgments about relative performance and how unusual results may be, one may also need to take into account differences in difficulty and other factors that are different from grade to grade.

Similarity Analyses

A very effective data forensics approach is to examine on a response by response level the answers given on each question in every subject for every possible pair or group of students who took the same examination or set of questions. This type of analysis can only be done for a substantial sized group when a data analyst has access to the data that emerge from scanning student answer sheets in a P&P setting and from item responses for individual students in a CBT environment.

Similarity analyses can only be carried out when one has access to the results of item responses, not merely the score results, for each student. This information permits you to determine how often the following situations occurred for all pairs of students:

- Number of times the two students answered the same questions correctly. For example, if student A had 25 questions correct in a section and Student B had 22, how many correct questions did they have in common?

- Number of identical incorrect answers

- Number of times that the same incorrect answers are chosen by students

- Number of changed answers (as determined by an inference that light but discernible marks represent original answers that were subsequently erased or by ascertaining from the computer record the sequence with which responses were recorded in CBT settings). Although it is possible to do responses for CBTs that are straightforward comparisons of answer changing, one is more likely to detect evidence of students receiving help during a test than to find "after the fact" answer changing that sometimes occurs with P&P.

A full similarity analysis uses these information elements and ratios of them to infer possible collaboration during an examination, possible shared assistance during an exam, or, in paper and pencil settings, changes made to both answer sheets after the test was completed.

A state incorporating similarity analyses into its procedures will need to determine when such analyses will be carried out. Two models can be identified – one is to conduct such analyses before scores are reported and the other is to wait until after scores are released. If the state carries out such analyses before reporting, it can then hold scores where there are concerns about validity because of testing irregularities.

When similarity analyses are conducted after score reporting it is not necessary to operate on as tight a schedule. Although timely follow up on possible testing irregularities is still very important, it will most frequently fall to schools to do the follow- up investigations. An exception is the situation where very extreme and pervasive anomalies in test results are judged to warrant action at the state level including the possibility of using third party investigators.

The act of withholding scores sends a strong message about the state's determination to provide fair and accurate assessment results. Once scores are reported, having to invalidate them has major consequences, and the fact that an investigation is going on can generate a great deal of media attention.

It should be noted that whereas similarity analyses can be performed in computer adaptive testing (CAT) settings, the number of identical questions taken by any pair of students will be limited by the size of the item pool. With large item pools and item selection rules that tend to encourage broad use of the item pool, the number of similar items may be small enough to significantly reduce the value of this approach for comparing any two students' results.

Erasure (Answer Changing) Analyses

Many states using P&P carry out some form of erasure analysis for their assessments. Similar analyses can also be done for CBT delivered exams where one can look at changes made by a student after first choosing an answer for a particular question. When there is a tip or an observation by a test monitor that there was an anomaly related to a particular class, actual answer sheets may be examined. The most common practice, though, is to rely on analyses based on the results of scanning answer sheets for paper and pencil administrations. The scanners employed for the millions of state assessments administered each year can have their sensitivity levels adjusted so that more than one mark can be detected for each question. Typically, the darkest mark is interpreted by a scoring program as the response that the student intended and lighter marks are interpreted as being "stray marks" such as smudges or previous answers that were erased.

There is a craft to using answer sheet erasures as one measure of possible testing irregularities that each state beginning this practice or refining what is already in place needs to either learn or bring in expertise to help their departmental staff. Testing vendors are the most readily available source of such help, but some academics and other researchers can also be helpful. One step in the wise use of erasure analysis is to determine the scope of erasures for an assessment program by subject and grade. One will find — if erasures have not already been investigated — that there are typically very few erasures per student per test. Even when schools emphasize the importance of students rechecking their work and using every minute of the testing period for this activity, the total number of erasures tends to be small, often one or less per student per test on average. So finding even as many as three or four per student per test may be a cause for concern.

When states devote major efforts to monitoring erasure analyses, they should develop, or have created for them, "erasure counts" at different levels – the entire state, districts, schools, and "classes" or the smallest units that their records permit. Generally these analyses are focused on detecting evidence of results suggesting adult involvement in inappropriate erasing and changing of answers. Even if only the total number of marks classified as erasures were the only bit of information that was compiled, it would prove very valuable in detecting possible misconduct. There are reasons why a single answer sheet will have many erasures. A student may have lost his or her place on an answer sheet and gone back to erase all the marks beyond the point when the student went off track to replace those marks with the ones the student believes to be the correct answers. Sometimes students smudge a section of their answer sheet and all the bubble areas that were impacted may be classified as having multiple marks. Most often, though, this type of marking is essentially random and will not have much of an impact on the totals even for a class, let alone school or district results. It is important to keep this possibility in mind, though, and to make clear to schools or classes that may warrant further investigation that the state is aware of this possibility and took it into account when interpreting erasure results.

In a P&P environment, studies of erasures are based on inferences drawn from the pattern of light and dark marks on answer sheets as opposed to inspection of actual answer sheets. In a CBT setting, there is information available about "answer changing" — the CBT equivalent of erasing. States need to build on experience and to draw on their vendors to interpret answer changing results in the CBT setting. In P&P state assessment settings, erasures are relatively rare, often averaging one erasure per subject test across all students and grades. In that context, even a relatively small number of erasures may well be indicative of a problem. This fact is often obscured by reports that focus on the statistical "unusualness" of results. The erasures for a class may be four standard deviations from the mean and yet reflect an average of three erasures per student per test subject. When answer change counts are created, they typically include the following:

- Total number of erasures;
- Total number of wrong to right erasures (often the most revealing bit of data in the event of misconduct);

- Total number of right to wrong erasures; and

- Total number of wrong to wrong erasures.

States or their vendors can then develop erasure statistics addressing such questions as what proportion of answer changes was from wrong to right. When a student changes a question for which their first answer was incorrect, he or she is choosing among three other possibilities when it is a four-choice multiple-choice question. If the student simply guessed at the answer, the student would only be right one third of the time. What if the students in a particular class moved to a correct answer more than 80% of the time, and what if that "success rate" was far greater than for all other classes in a school or state?

Answer Change Analyses for Computer-based Tests

The kinds of analyses and interpretations that states need to carry out for P&P also are applicable in some form to CBT. In order to get the maximum benefit from studying not erasures (as there are none), but answer changes, states and vendors will need to become knowledgeable about what constitutes "normal" answer changing in the CBT environment so that unusual behavior can be recognized and its significance evaluated. This is now more feasible than was the case a few years ago as states are increasingly making use of computer delivery either in their operational programs or through pilot projects. The principles and practices that have been employed in P&P can be used when analyzing responses to computer-delivered tests after taking into account the change in delivery mechanism. In CBT the comparison is between the first response chosen and subsequent choices. Testing systems can provide exact knowledge of any changes that were made so it is not necessary to infer what the student did from the lightness and darkness of marks on an answer sheet. If a particular student or set of students makes virtually all wrong to right changes, one needs to be very skeptical that the student was relying on his or her own knowledge and skills. Essentially states need to develop "rules of thumb" for evaluating the frequency and types of answer changing in the CBT environment.

Person Fit Analyses

One line of data forensics analyses for state assessment examines the consistency of students' responses across the questions on each test. In general, students perform best on the questions that most students find easy to answer, not quite as well on questions of moderate difficulty, and least well on the hardest questions on a test. If a student is very strong in a particular area such as mathematics, that student may answer correctly virtually all the easy and medium difficulty questions and miss only some of the hardest questions. Sometimes, however, the pattern for some of the students in a class does not adhere to this pattern, perhaps departing from it in very significant ways. One can find classes for which several students or an entire group does substantially better on the most difficult questions than on the less difficult ones.

What are possible legitimate reasons why such an outcome might be observed? Possibly the group was taught by a special instructional method that developed their skills in a quite different way than those of other students learning that subject in the state. Maybe the class contains many students who were educated in another country that approached the subject matter in a different way. Usually if such factors exist they are both known to instructional staff and are of a small enough impact that they do not lead to huge differences in students' profiles of knowledge.

There are a number of reasons why this pattern of unusual results might occur if the rules of testing were not being followed. If a teacher has obtained copies of actual test questions and used them in instruction, students may do much better on these questions regardless of how hard they are for students who did not receive such special coaching. Such a result can also occur if students received assistance during the administration of the test, despite direct statements in training materials for administrators that such assistance is impermissible.

Person fit analyses require access to student response data, not merely test scores. However, for the purpose of these analyses, it is not necessary to know what particular responses the student chose (as would be needed for conducting similarity analyses) or whether the student changed an answer (as is done with erasure analysis).

Person fit analyses provide very persuasive results when educator misbehavior has occurred and it is often easy to explain what the results mean to interested parties who have little to no training in testing. The approach can be applied to CBTs as well as P&P. In the case of CATs, unusual results of this nature can be viewed as "poor model fit." Rather than finding that all results appear to meet the model assumptions that item response theory (IRT) methods are based on, it appears that other dimensions of student performance are responsible in part for the observed results. Troublesome additional factors could include prior exposure to test questions or student copying, after the test event erasures, and the like.

Person fit analyses are not limited to multiple-choice test questions. Whenever a state has scored responses across sets of items, it can look for consistency across the test takers' responses. Inconsistencies that appear unrelated to the nature of the student's education and background are a red flag that merit further investigation.

Other Data Forensics Methods

There are other data forensics methods that are sometimes employed. In computer-delivered testing, analyses of response times to questions sometimes turn up instances of students responding to questions in less time than would be required to read a passage or comprehend a table. There are also methods that are slight variations of methods described above – counting the longest string of identical answers between two test takers, for example, as a form of similarity analysis, This same approach is fully applicable to computer delivered "fixed form" tests, but less powerful in CATs, because fewer items are likely to be in common for various pairs of students. There has also been research on "keyboard analytics" in computer-delivered testing to see if the responses of a test taker show the same type of keyboarding throughout an examination or whether it appears that two different respondents were involved in test taking.

Introducing Data Forensics to a State Assessment Program

There are critical initial steps that should be taken to pave the way for the introduction of data forensics into state assessment programs. For example, a policy regarding how results will be used is essential. Among the key questions that need to be answered are the following:

- What kinds of information will be routinely collected and analyzed?

- What results will trigger follow-up investigations or score holds if that is the practice that is adopted?

- Who will be asked to conduct investigations?

- What investigative procedures will be recommended or required?

- Who will have access to information about investigations and under what circumstances?

A state that is interested in introducing or expanding the role of data forensics in its assessment programs should address the issue of preparing local districts for this change, including developing a public information program — an issue covered in the next section of this chapter. The assessment director and his or her staff should seek out other state assessment directors who have been making substantial use of data forensics and get their advice on what methods to employ and how to use the results. It would also be advisable to draw on Technical Advisory Committee (TAC) members or university-based measurement professionals to help think through how the data forensics results will be used. It is not an issue of whether one will find cheating in your state assessment program — it is a virtual certainty that some level of cheating in your programs will be found. This has proved true for all state programs for which extensive data forensics have been performed. The time to think through how one will use the results is at the planning stage, not when the results are in hand.

B. Preparing Local Education Agencies for the Use of Data Forensics Information

Most K-12 educators and administrators have had very little training in educational measurement. Through their on-the-job experiences, they have learned how their state assessment programs are designed and are intended to function. There are annual training programs for the staff that function as school or district test coordinators and periodic briefings for principals and others who have administrative responsibility for state testing. Some school- and district-level administrators attend training that is primarily directed at test coordinators or the teachers who administer state tests. Even the most conscientious school administrators have little in the way of direct knowledge of data forensics or indeed of other psychometric approaches such as the process of equating by which the continuity of meaning of test scores over years is assured.

How can one help prepare district and school staff for the advent of the use of data forensics within a state? One of the first steps is to determine who needs what class of information. State staffs need also to think through, with the help of school staff, how that information can be presented to be most clearly understood. A letter or other communication to local education agency (LEA) leaders is one valuable step. Use existing training and communication channels such as district and school test coordinator training sessions. Consider also the development of a cadre of resource staff at the district level who are given thorough briefings and are provided with training materials for follow-up sessions at the school level. It is strongly recommended that school staffs not be led to believe that information from data forensics is easy to understand in the absence of specific instruction.

Data forensics is not easy to learn, but it is a valuable component of a fair and accurate testing program. State departments of education need to acknowledge the fact that the use of data forensics adds a burden to school staff and need to demonstrate their willingness to help with the task of learning this new approach to fairness and accuracy in testing.

Focus for the Use of Data Forensics in State Assessments

It is recommended that the explicit focus of data forensics analyses be reducing testing irregularities and thus enhancing the fairness and validity of state testing. It is not sufficient to merely report data forensics results to various jurisdictions down to the class and school level and ask for investigations of any anomalies. Under this model, if no improprieties were actually observed or reported, there is often no action taken even when the statistical results are strongly suggestive of problems.

It is a pleasure to note that some states make more productive uses of data forensics, incorporating the information obtained into the pre-score release period. At the same time as equating and other basic psychometric work is being performed, data forensics analyses are carried out and anomalous results evaluated. Based on results for the state as a whole, criteria are set for scores for individual schools and sometimes districts to be held until individual districts can investigate the findings. This approach is proving to be extremely effective in reducing the number of "flagged" test results year after year. In one state following this model, the number of scores being invalidated dropped 55 percent from one year to the next, a very dramatic decline.

Incorporating data forensics into the basic scoring and reporting cycle for a state is a major decision as there is typically a good deal of pressure to adhere to test score reporting deadlines. It is difficult to even entertain the idea of adding a component to the process. The consequences, on the other hand, of having undetected cheating that may be undermining the fairness and validity of test results and the integrity of a state assessment program warrant consideration of this possibility. One factor in states' willingness to consider more productive and timely uses of data forensics results may have been U.S. Secretary of Education Arne Duncan's policy letter to state educational leaders dated June 24, 2011, wherein he stated:

"I am writing to urge you to do everything you can to ensure the integrity of the data used to measure student achievement and ensure meaningful educational accountability in your state.

As I'm sure you know, even the hint of testing irregularities and misconduct in the test administration process could call into question school reform efforts and undermine the state accountability systems that you have painstakingly built over the past decade."

C. Legal and Regulatory Issues Regarding the Use of Data Forensics in State Assessments

The use of data forensics in state assessments is a relatively new phenomenon related to the increase in the stakes associated with state tests, so it seems reasonable to look to other testing settings that use statistical and psychometric data to make decisions about test takers or test administrators to infer how the courts or other relevant authorities might view such uses. In general, close attention has been paid to test user agreements entered into by test takers and to the regulations and directions that set the conditions for testing.

Turning first to test user agreements, it is critical that an assessment program be very clear and specific about the intended use of data forensics. In the testing that occurs in the U.S. military to ascertain the language proficiency of U.S. military personnel, signs appear in each testing room "Test Results are Subjected to Statistical Analyses" and "Cheating is a Violation of the Code of Military Justice." Test takers know that cheating on tests could result in discharge from the service and other penalties. In a similar manner, some states require teachers to affirm that they have followed all testing rules and cite possible penalties that could be applied to cheating on tests including loss of position and loss of one's teaching license.

As long as a state adheres to established regulations and procedures, the state is likely to be recognized as being within its sphere of power to take steps designed to ensure the fairness and appropriateness of test results. There is considerable variation from state to state as to how seriously cheating is viewed. In a 2011 case in New York State involving a paid impersonator taking the SAT, it was only possible to take legal action because the proxy test taker was paid for his actions. If the cheating had been for free, no statute classifying test cheating as a crime was on the books in the state (Lendon, 2011).

Even where test cheating is identified as a crime, the seriousness varies from that of a misdemeanor to a felony with related variation in the penalties that can be applied. In many cases the potential loss of one's position and teaching license are the most serious potential consequences.

V. FOLLOW-UP INVESTIGATIONS

Follow-up investigations of cheating and piracy of test questions on state assessments are addressed in this chapter. Specifically, the following areas are covered:

A. Level of Evidence Needed to Initiate an Investigation

B. Roles for State Level Staff, Districts, and Possible Outside Agencies

C. Model Investigations Kit

D. Timelines for Planning and Carrying Out Investigations

E. Highly Desirable Features of Follow-up Investigations for State Assessments

A. Level of Evidence Needed to Initiate an Investigation

One of the key decisions that must be made by any state department of education (DOE) is determining what level of evidence calls for an investigation. When there is a report from a school that educator misbehavior has occurred, proceeding with some form of investigation is a basic test program practice across many states. But what if the evidence is primarily statistical in nature — for example, very large increases in scores from one year to the next, high levels of wrong to right answer changes, or extremely similar response patterns for pairs or groups of students in one or more classes in a school?

While each state will need to make its own determination about what will be investigated, it is very strongly urged to spell out the rules that will be followed and then follow those rules scrupulously. If a state does not have well thought out investigation rules, critics may challenge the implementation. If a state has not specified what its practices are, it will be very vulnerable if it tries to take action even when misbehavior appears to have taken place.

B. Roles for State Level Staff, School Districts, and Possible Outside Agencies

States need to determine an overall strategy for managing investigations. It is frequently the case that states ask districts to carry out the initial investigation of any reported or suspected testing irregularity regardless of the origin of the concern. In some instances, states play major roles in investigations either through the participation of state staff or by issuing comprehensive and explicit guidelines regarding how investigations are to be conducted and the nature of reports required from local education agencies (LEAs).

The DOE needs to identify a person with lead responsibility for follow-up investigations. This can be a staff member from the assessment group or maybe another area, such as accountability or legal. In states where there are relatively few staff in assessment, this may be an assignment to be carried out along with other responsibilities. If data forensics analyses are performed, the state needs to expect that there will be evidence of irregularities at every major administration.

In larger departments, the management of follow-up investigations will likely become a full-time position, even if it does not start that way.

The lead state person will need to draw on psychometric, operational, legal, and communications staff to develop follow-up investigations. In the next section of this chapter, the development of an investigations kit for use by school districts is proposed. One way of arranging for the multiple state-level perspectives that are needed is to form a committee that represents the different areas and individuals that should be involved.

School districts that are asked to carry out investigations also need to assign a lead person. The choice of such a person and the location within the district's administrative structure should take into account the extent and nature of the testing irregularities that have occasioned the follow-up investigation. If testing in only one or a few classes needs to be reviewed, the level of staff member involved can be different than if multiple schools across the district need to be investigated. In such cases, it will be especially important to keep the local superintendent's office and the school board informed of plans for the follow-up investigation.

If the state has provided clear directions for the kind of investigation and report that is expected, the task will be much more manageable. In every instance, the district will need to bring together the available information. It is usually relatively easy to access student, class, and school test data relevant to a follow-up investigation, so the lead district person need not be an assessment staff member. However, the perspective of assessment staff will still be needed to evaluate the results that are available.

If a state or school district needs to conduct investigations of widespread testing anomalies or ones that are highly suggestive of inappropriate behavior by educators, consideration should be given to bringing in experts from outside the school district. In such circumstances, the credentials and relevant experience of the experts should be checked. State assessment staff from other states can be a very helpful source of background information about employing investigation strategies.

C. Model Investigations Kit

One of the most helpful steps that state DOEs can take to enhance the quality of school district follow-up investigations is to prepare an investigations kit covering the following:

- Assigning Responsibilities
- Reviewing the State's Directive to Investigate
- Reviewing Available Information
- Planning and Conducting Interviews
- Preparing Interview Questions
- Developing a Report

Assigning Responsibilities

The investigations kit should provide the state's perspective on the appropriate placement of responsibility for a follow-up investigation. The assignment will be based in part on the nature and severity of the problems detected. Should responsibility be primarily placed on a school principal, on a central office supervisor, or with a school staff member with existing state assessment responsibilities such as a district or school test coordinator? Whatever the choice, district and school staff should be informed of the assignment and its dimensions, how much authority is being delegated, and how school staff can obtain clarification of the expectations that the district has about cooperation in the investigation.

Reviewing the State's Directive to Investigate

What is the state asking for in the way of an investigation and what information is being provided? If a "tip" was received by the state or a central school district office, what was the nature of that tip? Were specific educators mentioned by name? Is the problem described as occurring on one specific testing occasion or is the charge that there has been pervasive misbehavior? What exactly is the state asking to receive from the district as a result of the investigation? In some instances, typically rare ones, the irregularities may occur across multiple schools and be very troublesome. In those circumstances, moving the investigation directly to central office management is recommended. In most settings, the initial investigation should occur at the school level.

Reviewing Available Information

How much detail has the state or a tipster provided about testing anomalies? Have unusual test results been identified? If so, for which grades, subjects, and classes? Are comparison data being provided that help characterize the "unusualness" of particular testing outcomes? Can the district use its own data sets to evaluate the unusualness of particular test results? Interpretation of test results should be done conservatively. The goal is to identify and take action against clear evidence of potential testing misbehaviors.

Planning and Conducting Interviews

Individuals who are called upon to conduct interviews need to be trained for that purpose. They need to understand the requirements of the state, any school district rules that apply, and the general context provided by the Family Educational Rights and Privacy Act (FERPA) to protect the privacy of student data as well as other regulations and legislation directed at honoring the rights of all involved in investigations. The particular forms to be used and the procedures for requesting interviews and recording results need to be quite clear. Can a student, teacher, or administrator who is to be interviewed have someone, such as an attorney or a union representative, accompany them during an interview? Who will have access to the results of the interviews and on what schedule?

Preparing Interview Questions

Each state is likely to choose to use its own set of interview questions and those questions can be expected to vary depending on the particular testing anomalies that prompted the investigation. If the follow up was stimulated by a very large jump in scores for a group as opposed to a credible report about students receiving assistance answering test questions, then different questions will be appropriate.

Following is a list of all of the types of questions that warrant consideration when developing an interview guide for a particular investigation:

- Were you asked to read the manual for administering the test?

- Were you provided with security training? When and by whom?

- When did testing materials arrive at a school? In the case of computer based tests (CBTs), when did you first have access to the examination questions?

- Where were physical test materials stored?

- Who had access to the test materials in both pencil and paper (P&P) and CBT delivered exams?

- Describe the process on test day for the school as a whole and for each testing room.

- How were test materials collected and mailed from the school when testing was complete?

- Did you observe any testing irregularities in your school on any of the testing days?

- Are there ways that you would like to see test security practices enhanced?

Developing a Report

When providing advice regarding developing an investigation report, the state should be explicit about the information that is being sought and about the level of detail that is needed. Is it sufficient to note that staff received training in test administration techniques at district and school test coordinator sessions or are specific details required? More documentation will better serve the state when developing a report, and in the case of any subsequent personnel action or litigation.

The key finding of a report needs to be highlighted and a description provided if the investigation uncovered security shortcomings. For example, what were the security shortcomings? How did the school district deal with them or plan to address them in the future (e.g., changes to training and monitoring procedures for state assessments)?

D. Timelines for Planning and Carrying Out Investigations

If a state does not already have a plan for carrying out follow-up investigations, it should do so as soon as possible. Once substantial anomalies or reports of inappropriate testing behaviors surface, investigations will have to be launched and quickly. If a plan has not been developed in advance, procedures will have to be created in a very short period and may not stand up to the close scrutiny to which they will very likely be subjected.

If the state has the opportunity to proceed in a measured fashion, these stages and specified timelines are recommended for developing a plan:

- Development of a plan for review – At least one month

- Notification of school districts about the plan and their responsibilities, request for feedback – At least two months

- Review of feedback, revision, and provisional use – At least two months

- Operational use and review – At least one testing cycle

It would be easy to call for multi-month development and review stages, leading up to having a formal and approved investigations plan, but it is doubtful that this would be realistic in most circumstances. Many states already have some procedures in place and the key task will be to integrate what already exists into a single plan and to get reviews from state and district staff, technical advisors, and key vendors.

Once an investigation plan is in place, how long should investigations take? One factor is the extent of the irregularities detected or reported via a "tip." If only a single class is involved, one to two months are likely to be sufficient. If a larger group is involved and there is evidence suggestive of a coordinated and group effort, three to four months may be needed. This is not a process to rush as important decisions will be required if misbehavior is confirmed.

E. Highly Desirable Features of Follow-up Investigations for State Assessments

Based on our experiences, there are a number of highly desirable features of state investigative processes that we have observed:

- Attention is focused on improving security in the future – There is some tendency to approach follow-up security investigations with what might be called a prosecutorial model: "Let's find every possible example of a testing misbehavior and take action against the responsible party." Much as one can be strongly in favor of promoting test security, this approach can be perceived to be counter-productive by some. It fosters an adversarial atmosphere and can, and has, led to the condemnation of many teachers and administrators through "guilt by association."

- The "worst-of-the-worst" receive the most attention – It is critical to pursue the most egregious cases so thoroughly that any reasonable individual who looked at the evidence that led to the state taking action would most likely recognize and understand the state's decisions. One guideline to follow is to establish what is covered in criminal investigations under the heading "motive, means, and opportunity." Who would gain from high student test scores? Who had access to the test copy in advance and could have provided the content to students? Who had access to the place where tests and answer sheets were stored?

- Other possible explanations are seriously considered – The most thorough review of statistical findings and other evidence is conducted with attention to the possibility that there is an explanation for anomalous results that is unrelated to misbehavior by students or staff. This is a challenging position to take and sustain as the first response to the suggestion that there may have been inappropriate testing behavior is almost always one of these:

  - "Impossible."

  - "Not in my school."

  - "Not Mr. X. or Ms. Y."

- Investigators sustain an "innocent until proven guilty" perspective and are firm with their questions – The mere fact that investigators are told over and over about exemplary practices in planning and delivering instruction that students had received before taking the state assessments should not settle the issue for investigators. How plausible are the results? How do the results for a class or school compare with past results for the same school and results for other classes and schools?

- Multiple lines of evidence are used – One of the most valuable aids to an investigator is the possession of multiple types of test security related information spanning many years.

VI. SUMMARY AND RECOMMENDATIONS

In this final chapter, a summary of the guidebook is provided along with some key conclusions. Lastly, recommendations to states on improving test security and next steps for them to take are highlighted. The chapter addresses the following:

A. Summary and Conclusions

B. Critical Recommendations to States

A. Summary and Conclusions

Test security is increasingly important to states and others involved in assessment. More effective security is needed to ensure the integrity, validity, and fairness of state assessment programs. In order to achieve this, the Technical Issues in Large-Scale Assessment (TILSA) Test Security project was initiated in 2012 to assist states and others with a resource that can help them enhance their security procedures and practice. This guidebook places an emphasis on providing guidance, advice, and examples of useful information and materials. The work on this project was a true collaboration of the authors, states, testing organizations, and the Council of Chief State School Officers.

Based on the data collected as part of this project from the TILSA survey of states, it is obvious that states want more information on ways to improve security for their assessments. Most states have had to deal with test security breaches. All states have found firm evidence of cheating by teachers or school administrators. States expressed concerns about expanded testing windows, the use of technology for cheating purposes, the posting of secure materials (i.e., test items) by students of other states on the Internet, and the potential of evildoers to hack into computers to access tests or test data. Almost all states agree that it is very important to improve their policies and procedures, have better training, conduct better oversight of test administration, and have better budgets for the test security work needed in their state.

The guidebook is intended to help states deal with these issues. As noted earlier, the main purpose is to serve as a resource for states to use to prevent and detect state assessment irregularities such as cheating and test piracy and to investigate suspected or confirmed examples of improper or unethical testing behavior by either students or educators. The guidebook focuses on three main test security issues: prevention, detection, and follow-up investigations. Discussion and details of security practices within the three topics include the following:

1. Prevention – Standards for the test security aspects of the design, development, and operation of state assessment programs, both paper and pencil and computer-based programs (with an emphasis on the latter), for both multiple choice response and performance measures.

2. Detection – Guidelines for planning, implementing, and interpreting data forensics analyses.

3. Follow-Up Investigations – Strategies for planning and conducting investigations and actions that states may need to take based on findings from investigations.

Each of these chapters provides a wealth of information that states can use to improve their policies and procedures, and implement a best practices approach to test security. For prevention, states can refer to existing test security standards, adopt test security checklists for their program, and consider the role of an audit of their security procedures. These activities are intended to identify security vulnerabilities and recommend remedies for states to implement.

For detection, states can learn more about data forensics methods and the strengths and weaknesses of each – for example, gains analysis, similarity analysis, erasure analysis, aberrance or person fit, and other methods. They can use this information to then prepare their districts on the use of the information that comes from a data forensics analyses. Case studies and legal/regulatory issues related to this method are described.

For follow-up investigations, states have more information on what level of evidence is needed to initiate an investigation, the roles of state and district staff, desirable features of state-initiated follow-up investigations, and a model investigations kit to review and use as a resource.

In addition to the information contained in these three chapters, many more resources are provided in the guidebook's appendices. States can refer to these documents and use what they want to further improve the security of their assessment programs.

B. Critical Recommendations to States

There are many recommendations throughout this guidebook. It seems reasonable, though, to list a limited number of critical recommendations for each of the three aspects of test security: prevention, detection, and follow-up investigation.

Prevention

- Devote as much attention as possible to prevention, even using announcements that you will be taking multiple steps to encourage adherence to testing rules and to discourage misbehavior. Include in your public outreach the consequences of failing to adhere to the rules of state testing.

- Assign responsibility for test security and monitor the effectiveness of the state's efforts.

- Limit testing windows to the extent feasible.

- Provide security training to all staff, both when they move into jobs and periodically to be sure they are current on security policies and procedures.

Detection

- Have your plans for employing data forensics reviewed and evaluated from a legal and a communications perspective.

- Employ data forensics analyses regularly for all high stakes programs. Use several different data forensics approaches, appropriate to the type of assessment program you are administering. The magnitude of score improvement will be a valuable indicator regardless of the type of program you have. Other analyses will depend on the program. For example, erasure analyses are recommended for paper and pencil examinations and analyses of time spent on items are recommended for computer-based tests.

- Develop interpretive guidelines for using data forensics analyses as a basis for action and include in staff training the interpretation and use of data forensics results.

Follow-Up Investigation

- Be conservative when interpreting and acting on data forensics results. Do not act on every statistically significant finding. Investigate and move on the "worst of the worst." Consider all in-depth investigations as efforts to clarify results, not attempts to prove people guilty.

- When a decision is made that the data forensics merit an in-depth investigation, always respect the privacy and professionalism of all individuals involved in the investigation.

- Maintain comprehensive records of any investigations in a form suitable for sharing in a court of law.

REFERENCES

American Educational Research Association (AERA), American Psychological Association (APA), and National Council on Measurement in Education (NCME) Joint Committee on Standards for Educational and Psychological Testing. (1999). *Standards for educational and psychological testing.* Washington DC: AERA.

The American National Standards Institute (ANSI). (2010). *Accreditation program for personnel certification bodies under ANSI/ISO/IEC 17024* [certification program]. Washington, DC: Author. Retrieved December 18, 2012, from https://www.ansica.org/wwwversion2/outside/PERgeneral.asp?menuID=2.

Caveon™Test Security. (2012). *Test security standards – Topics only.* http://www.caveon.com: Author.

Cizek, G.J. (1999). *Cheating on tests: How to do it, detect it, and prevent it.* Mahwah, New Jersey: Lawrence Erlbaum Associates, Inc.

Council of Chief State School Officers (CCSSO) and the Association of Test Publishers (ATP). (2010). *Operational best practices for statewide large-scale assessment programs.* Washington, DC: Author. Retrieved December 18, 2012, from http://www.ccsso.org/resources/publications/operational_best_practices_for_statewide_large-scale_assessment_programs.html.

Hanover Research. (2012). *State- and district-level academic dishonesty policies.* Washington, DC: CCSSO.

Lendon, B. (2011, September 28). *7 arrested in alleged SAT cheating scam* [CNN web log post]. Retrieved December 18, 2012, from http://news.blogs.cnn.com/2011/09/28/7-arrested-in-alleged-sat-cheating-scam/.

NCME. (2012). *Testing and data integrity in the administration of statewide student assessment programs.* Madison, WI: Author. Retrieved December 20, 2012, from http://ncme.org/default/assets/File/Committee%20Docs/Test%20Score%20Integrity/Test%20Integrity-NCME%20Endorsed%20%282012%20FINAL%29.pdf.

Vega, J. (2012) *Academic cheating bilks the test of time.* College Times, Published November 5, 2010, Updated November 6, 2012. www.ecollegetimes.com/student-life/academic-cheating-bilks-the-test-of-time-1.2788888

Wollack, J.A., & Fremer, J.J. (Eds.). (2013). [book will be available March 27]. *Handbook of test security.* New York City, NY: Routledge.

RESOURCES

The American National Standards Institute
http://www.ansi.org/

Association of Test Publishers (ATP) Security Council
http://www.testpublishers.org/

Caveon Test Security
http://www.caveon.com

CCSSO/ATP *Operational Best Practices for Statewide Large-Scale Assessment Programs* (2010)
http://www.ccsso.org/resources/publications/operational_best_practices_for_statewide_large-scale_assessment_programs.html

Data Forensics Summit at University of Kansas
http://www.cete.us/conference2012/

International Test Commission Guidelines on Test Security
http://www.intestcom.org/guidelines

NCES Special Symposium on Test Integrity
http://ies.ed.gov/whatsnew/conferences/?id=966&cid=2

NCES Report on Testing Integrity "Issues and Recommendations for Best Practice"
http://nces.ed.gov/pubsearch/pubsinfo.asp?pubid=2013454

NCME White Paper on Test Integrity
http://ncme.org/default/assets/File/Committee%20Docs/Test%20Score%20Integrity/Test%20Integrity-NCME%20Endorsed%20%282012%20FINAL%29.pdf

U.S. Department of Education (USED) Request for Information (RFI) on Testing Integrity
https://www.federalregister.gov/articles/2012/01/17/2012-753/request-for-information-to-gather-technical-expertise-pertaining-to-testing-integrity#p-3

APPENDICES

APPENDIX A. Acknowledgments

This research project benefited from the support and advice of members of the Council of Chief State School Officers' Technical Issues in Large-Scale Assessment (TILSA) State Collaborative on Assessment and Student Standards (SCASS). The authors want to especially thank Charlene Tucker, Doug Rindone, and Duncan MacQuarrie for their advice and support, and the workgroup members for their work and participation.

In addition, the project wishes to acknowledge the excellent work of Gregory Cizek, University of North Carolina, who served as a reviewer of the final draft.

TILSA Test Security Workgroup Members

Charlie Bruen – Arizona

Juan D'Brot and Nate Hixon – West Virginia

Roger Ervin – Kentucky

Dianne Henderson-Montero – ETS

Laura Kramer – University of Kansas

Abe Krist – Connecticut

Doug Levin – SETDA

Leah McGuire – Measured Progress

Jim Palmer – Illinois

Gary Phillips – AIR

Patricia Reiss – Hawaii

Joe Saunders and Doug Alexander – South Carolina

Steve Viger – Michigan

Charlie Wayne – Pennsylvania

Carsten Wilmes – WIDA Consortium

Max Xu – Ohio

APPENDIX B. Glossary of Test Security Terms

Since language and terminology may be used differently from state to state, some of the most commonly used terms in this guidebook are defined below:

Breach
(1) an event, intentional or not, that results in the inappropriate exposure of test items or answers that could potentially impact the accuracy of the test results; OR

(2) an action by others before, during, or after a test administration to impact student test scores (e.g., educators changing student answer sheets).

Cheating
General term that can include educator or student misconduct or improprieties that includes intentional misbehavior or unethical practices. Note that this term is not used in every state. Some states avoid the use of the word "cheating" in their communications and use different terminologies.

Compromise
Disclosure of test items or forms; can be intentional or unintentional. May also refer to changing the interpretation of a test score or changing the test score itself.

Data Forensics
The use of analytic methods to identify or detect possible cheating. Procedures can include evaluation of score gains, aberrance or person fit, erasures, latency analysis, similarity analysis, and examination of changes in student responses (wrong-to-right, right-to-wrong, wrong-to-wrong).

Impropriety
Inappropriate misconduct; a more serious offense than an irregularity. The difference between impropriety and irregularity is usually defined in perception of the degree, intent, and/or effect of the misconduct.

Irregularity
This includes many different activities, not necessarily cheating, but anything unusual that happened during testing, such as the fire alarms went off or a power outage.

Misconduct
Misbehavior during testing, such as inappropriate proctoring or other violations of standard testing protocol.

Security Investigation
Follow-up activities regarding possible cheating or piracy of test materials. Typically involves the collection of evidence, review of available information, interviews of suspected staff, and summary of findings from the investigation.

Test Piracy

Stealing of test forms, items, prompts, or other secure testing materials, often for the purpose of selling the materials to others.

Test Security Kit

A document for states that may provide instructions about a state's security-related procedures, processes, and regulations, including the escalation path to be followed in the event of a test security breach.

APPENDIX C. Caveon Test Security Standards

Caveon™ Test Security

Test Security Standards – Topics Only

May 2012

> Each organization should create and maintain a Security Plan, which is a formal, written document that contains the goals of the program, policies and procedures, definitions, roles and responsibilities, the Security Incident Response Plan, approvals, and other components and content as covered below.

Section One: Security Plan

1.1.   A written, complete Security Plan exists.

1.2.   Management approves the Security Plan.

1.3.   The Security Plan is available to all stakeholders.

1.4.   The Security Plan contains all necessary components.

1.5.   The content of the Security Plan is comprehensive.

1.6.   The Security Plan is reviewed regularly.

> There are many individuals involved in protecting the security of a program's tests. The roles and responsibilities of these individuals should be identified and communicated to prevent any weakness in the overall security.

Section Two: Roles and Responsibilities

2.1.   Security roles and associated responsibilities have been identified.

2.2.   Training is provided to make all individuals understand their roles and responsibilities.

2.3.   All individuals have been provided with a security manual (or the portion that applies to them) that describes the security procedures for which they are responsible.

2.4.   Back-up resources for critical roles have been identified.

Section Three: Budget and Funding

> **Organizations need to establish and maintain a budget and contingency funding for security purposes.**

3.1.   The cost of security is included in the program's budget.

3.2.   The amount budgeted for security purposes is sufficient.

3.3.   The amount budgeted includes outsourcing costs.

3.4.   The budget is reviewed regularly.

3.5.   The ROI for security costs has been determined.

Section Four: Legal Precautions

> **The security of an organization depends to a large extent on how well prepared the organization is from a legal point of view.**

4.1.   All content contributors, whether employees, volunteers or contractors, have entered legal agreements that transfer ownership of the items, tests and related materials to the organization.

4.2.   All individuals or organizations that have access to items, tests and other sensitive material are required to enter a legal agreement that prohibits disclosure.

4.3.   The organization takes steps to establish and maintain legal protection of tests, items, results, examinee information and other sensitive test information.

4.4.   All examinees, including beta or field test participants, enter a test-use agreement prior to testing which incorporates the program's testing rules.

4.5.   The test-use agreement or its elements are made available to examinees prior to testing in program information and by other means.

4.6.   Testing service providers, including test development and delivery providers, distributors, testing site operators, data management vendors, test readers/recorders etc., enter vendor agreements.

Section Five: Test and Item Design

> **Tests and items should be designed, as much as possible, for security purposes. The design should discourage memorization and sharing and make common methods of cheating less effective. They should limit item exposure, thereby prolonging the usefulness of items and test results.**

5.1.   Test design allows item exposure to be monitored, calculated, and controlled.

5.2.   An item bank exists that is large enough to provide multiple equivalent forms and items that are interchangeable.

5.3.   An item bank update policy, rules, and schedule exist.

5.4.   A process exists that allows items or tests to be replaced in a test as soon as compromise is detected or normal exposure levels are reached.

5.5.   The effectiveness of item exposure control methods in reducing item exposure has been established.

5.6.   Test construction strategies that reduce or control item exposure are being used.

5.7.   Other test and item design features are used to discourage memorization, copying, and sharing.

5.8.   Security-based test and item designs are compatible with test development tools, test delivery platforms, data management systems, and item analysis procedures.

Section Six: Test Development and Maintenance

> **It is important that during the development of items and tests that the content is protected, both through the use of agreements as well as sound security procedures.**

6.1.   Computers used by program personnel are password protected and not connected to Internet.

6.2.   An administrator controls and monitors access to item banks and test development systems.

6.3.   All copies of the item bank, groups of items, tests, or individual items, produced as part of the development process are deleted when no longer needed.

6.4.   Items not developed in a secure database are submitted to the database, transmitted by secure means, and later deleted by the contributor when development work is complete.

6.5. Secure beta or pilot testing is used to qualify original and replacement items and to create tests.

6.6. For security purposes, an item development and use management plan exists to ensure that the item bank has sufficient items in the event of a security incident or normal overexposure of items.

Section Seven: Test Publication

After the test has been created it is published and distributed. Security measures must be in place to protect it during this period.

7.1. The test files and published test are kept in a secure area.

7.2. The length of time that tests and item banks are possessed by testing sites should be closely monitored and controlled when their use is infrequent.

Section Eight: Test Administration

Tests need to remain secure immediately before, during, and after test administration. Test administration refers to the process of registering examinees, scheduling, providing physical security measures, presenting the test content, gathering the test results, and communicating results and other information to the organization.

8.1. Well-defined and appropriate methods of intervention are used when suspicious activity occurs.

8.2. Proctors and other test administration personnel are trained in procedures to be followed when suspicious activity is discovered.

8.3. Test administrators and proctors are not instructors, trainers, or other individuals with knowledge of the exam content.

8.4. Tests are administered in a location separate from training activities.

8.5. Proper identification procedures are followed.

8.6. A list of individuals prohibited from test registration and administration is maintained and referenced at appropriate times to deny access.

8.7. Examinees are continuously monitored during test administration through use of proctors, biometrics, video cameras, etc. (This is a service usually provided by the test delivery provider.)

8.8.   Examinees are informed that they are being monitored at all times during their exam and of other security measures.

8.9.   Physical control is exercised during testing over unauthorized material and devices.

8.10.   Physical control, both distribution and retrieval, is exercised during testing over material that is usually permitted to be used to make certain that the method of use is within program guidelines.

8.11.   Authorized material that is not used is securely stored and destroyed when it is no longer needed.

8.12.   A process is in place to report any discrepancies in test administration. (For example, if a test is taken under non-standard conditions.)

8.13.   A Tip Line or other contact information is provided to examinees to report suspicious activity before, during, or after testing.

8.14.   All relevant data from the test administration, including test results, discrepancy reports, and suspicious activity reports, are immediately forwarded to the test sponsor or test sponsor contractor, as required.

8.15.   A retake policy exists that is designed to reduce item exposure.

Section Nine: Test Scores and Results

Test scores should be subjected to a security analysis to validate their usefulness for subsequent decisions. In addition, the accuracy of the scoring process, from a security perspective, should be verified.

9.1.   Procedures exist for detecting and evaluating suspicious test scores.

9.2.   The accuracy of each score is confirmed.

9.3.   The accuracy of other test results is confirmed.

Section Ten: Physical Security

Tests, and the systems and materials needed to develop tests, must be secure in a testing program's facilities during every phase of the test production process.

10.1. An individual within the organization is assigned managerial responsibility for the physical security of test development materials and areas where materials are used and stored.

10.2. Work and storage areas are designed or configured for secure use of test materials during work hours.

10.3. Electronic item banking systems and other test development systems and databases are secured.

10.4. Test materials are only removed from the testing program facilities with specific authorization by personnel with appropriate training regarding the secure transportation and use of materials at remote locations.

10.5. Test development materials are collected and destroyed at the conclusion of each test development process.

10.6. In the event of an unforeseen emergency, such as a fire, flood or power failure, all storage and work areas where sensitive test materials are used or stored should, to the extent possible, be physically monitored and secured before the facilities are vacated.

Section Eleven: Information Security

> **Digital and physical information related to the organization's testing program must be stored and transmitted securely at all times.**

11.1. Policies and procedures exist for security during transmission of test materials (test documents, item pools, and examinee databases).

11.2. Copies of all test materials are kept and stored securely.

11.3. An action plan is in place to investigate transmission and shipping discrepancies and errors.

11.4. Modification of electronic information and test materials occurs according to established policy and procedures.

11.5. Information regarding test results and examinees is shared in a manner consistent with policies and procedures that protect the integrity of the information and the rights of the examinees.

11.6. The program's testing data are reviewed regularly to detect security compromises and their effects on the exams, scores, and program decisions made.

Section Twelve: Web and Media Monitoring

> **With the Internet's ubiquity, it is critical that a high-stakes testing program monitor the Web for the disclosure of its copyrighted items and other test information.**

12.1.   The Internet and other media are monitored regularly for suspicious activity or the sharing of copyrighted information.

12.2.   Routine reports are provided that include findings and recommendations.

12.3.   Monitoring activities are reviewed and evaluated for effectiveness.

12.4.   Monitoring is used to evaluate the effectiveness of security measures taken.

12.5.   Printed and computer-based test preparation materials, and other training materials, are routinely reviewed for disclosure of test content.

Section Thirteen: Security Awareness and Training

> **The program should take proper steps to place the value of a security plan and specific security problems into perspective, and to disclose and use security information carefully.**

13.1.   Identified security vulnerabilities in the program are being addressed.

13.2.   Security vulnerabilities are routinely evaluated for improvement.

13.3.   All program personnel and contractors receive appropriate training in components of the security plan and associated security policies and procedures that are relevant to their roles and responsibilities.

13.4.   The positioning of security incidents is dealt with carefully and confidentially within the organization.

Section Fourteen: Security Incident Response Plan

> **The organization has a plan for responding to known security incidents. This response may involve further investigation and evaluation of compliance by the individuals or organizations involved. The plan also includes appropriate and measured responses to the incident.**

14.1.   An Action Plan exists that covers a comprehensive set of test abuse activities.

14.2.   Appropriate sanctions are specified for each type of test abuse.

14.3.   Decision-making criteria, procedures and evidence requirements controlling the imposition of sanctions are specified.

14.4.   Possible sanctions are communicated in advance to individuals and organizations.

14.5.   An individual or committee is organized and empowered to review allegations of test abuse and impose sanctions.

14.6.   An appeal process is in place.

14.7.   A record is kept of test abuse allegations and all actions taken, along with appeals.

14.8.   Evidence is gathered in a manner which will assure its utility for subsequent legal action.

14.9.   Periodic reviews of internal and outsourced processes are evaluated for compliance with the Security Plan.

14.10.. Imposed sanctions are publicized in a manner which protects the identity of the effected individuals and (where appropriate) organizations.

Section Fifteen: Managing Security Investigations

An organization should have a concrete plan for responding to actual or alleged security incidents. This response may involve further investigation and evaluation of compliance with policies and procedures by the individuals or organizations involved, as well as appropriate and measured responses to the actual or alleged incident.

15.1   Responsibility for managing the security investigation process has been clearly defined.

15.2   Investigation procedures have been piloted before they are used operationally.

15.3   Investigation procedures have received reviews from the perspective of program managers, measurement staff, communications staff, and legal staff.

15.4   Sufficient funds have been allocated to permit thorough investigations.

15.5   Where initial investigations are to be conducted by test administrators as is often the case with state assessment programs, an Investigations Kit has been developed that spells out procedures to be followed, records to be kept, and laws and regulations that must be followed, such as those protecting the privacy of the test takers and administrators and the confidentiality of test materials.

APPENDIX D. Example Outline and Description of a Test Security Manual

State department of education (DOE) staff will need to decide on what policies, procedures, and materials need to be included in a test security manual or handbook. One important source of information may be information from a security audit of the testing activities of the DOE if one was conducted in the state. A security audit report will have recommended security enhancements in a number of areas, many of which are typically covered in a security handbook. Thus, a security handbook will likely parallel a security audit in its coverage.

Therefore, the proposed outline of the content for a test security manual should include detailed information on the following topics:

- Roles and Responsibilities
- Budgeting and Finance
- Legal
- Test Distribution
- Test Administration
- Test Scores and Results
- Information Security
- Internet Monitoring
- Security Awareness and Training
- Security Breach Action Plan
- Physical Security
- Conducting Security Investigations

Of course, states are empowered to include different sections if they choose. This list is a starting point for a manual. In addition to providing a centralized document where all state policies and practices related to test security can be kept and maintained, the test security manual can also serve as a historical document for referring to any audits, forensics analyses, or investigations that have been conducted in the state.

All areas of interest need to be covered in a manner conducive to training new staff and in maintaining up-to-date descriptions of policies and procedures. For some purposes, following the chronological path of testing through test administration and beyond is a useful structuring device. In other instances, however, such as the management of security breach investigations, it may be more useful to focus on the roles of not only DOE assessment staff, but the roles of human resources, information technology, financial, and legal staff.

In summary, a test security manual should provide

- An electronic document based on the results of the security audit, further review of DOE documents, and additional interviews

- A single, comprehensive source defining procedures, processes, and regulations, including the escalation path to be followed in the event of a test security investigation

- A flexible means to document the most critical processes related to the testing activities of the DOE

APPENDIX E. Example of Data Forensics Information for Requests for Proposals

This appendix provides an example of language that could be used in requests for proposals (RFPs) to encourage vendors to propose the use of data forensics analyses in state assessment programs.

Data Forensics Analysis of Test Results for Potential Testing Irregularities

Bidder is expected to provide solutions employing data forensics statistical analyses to evaluate whether test results on select assessment tools were earned fairly. The integrity of the state's assessment system depends on adherence to rules governing the program in the preparation of students, test administration, and the handling of assessment tool materials both before and upon completion of testing. The State is specifically interested in determining whether

- There is evidence of collusion among test takers

- There are results indicative of prior exposure to test questions

- Students are responding consistently across the test materials

- Answer changes follow the expected pattern for students working independently and with no coaching or outside influence

- Changes in performance from test event to test event are consistent with what might be expected given a conscientious effort to help students learn

Requirements: Bidders are to submit delivery schedules for analyses in terms of the length of time between receipt of data and submission of reports. Further, bidders are to submit samples of data forensics reports illustrating how the results can be used by the state. Proposals that are responsive to this requirement's request should include

- Detailed specifications of the statistical analyses used to provide the data forensics analyses

- Demonstration of multiple methods to be used in analyzing results

- Demonstration of the proposed data forensics analysis solution as used by other state departments of education analyzing test results

- Demonstrations of in-depth knowledge of the state's assessment examinations (or similar examinations), with the relevant security regulations, and with the specific security guidelines that test administrators, typically classroom teachers, are trained to follow

New bidders are to identify each assessment component to be analyzed, detail the procedures to conduct said analysis, and provide the costs for annual implementations of analysis. At time of contracting for services, the State will determine the assessments for analyzing and the periodicity of analyses. Bidders will assume that forensic analyses are to include all applicable grades and content areas.

Deliverables: The State will expect a written report of the results of the data forensics analyses. The areas to be covered in the report should include at least the following:

- Description of the methodology employed

- Indications of how the results are intended to be used (e.g., what do the findings mean and what further investigation is recommended)

- Number and percent of statistically inconsistent results, by test and grade

- Specific schools showing inconsistent results

- Types of inconsistencies observed and extent to which schools exhibited more than one type

- If feasible, names of specific students with inconsistent results

- Impact of inconsistencies on student performance – how greatly did the inconsistencies impact "passing rates," for example

- Evidence of compromise of exams (e.g., how many items appear to have been compromised, what appears to have been the impact on test taker performance)

- Specific items that appear to have been compromised

- Recommendations for possible additional psychometric analyses to confirm that scores were earned fairly and in a manner consistent with assessment policies and regulations

The contractor will be required to keep all results confidential, so that the State can use and release the results in a manner it judges appropriate. The contractor, moreover, will be expected to provide consultation as requested as the results are reviewed at the department level and in the course of any subsequent investigations. Additional requests for analyses may be made to the contractor. If the contractor has the capacity to help with detailed investigations of statistical inconsistencies, at the district and school level, the nature of the assistance that can be provided should be indicated in the response to this request.

References: A response to this specific activity is to include a list of contact names for references about past data forensics analyses, including an indication of the kind of analyses performed.

APPENDIX F. Sample Security Investigations Kit

State departments of education (DOEs) may want to enhance the quality of school district follow-up investigations by preparing a security investigations kit, which should, at a minimum, include information on the critical issues and questions listed below. Following is an outline of a sample investigations kit with key topics that should be addressed:

A. Assigning responsibilities

   1. What is the state's perspective on the appropriate placement of responsibility for a follow-up investigation?

   2. Should responsibility be primarily placed on a school principal, on a central office supervisor, or with a school staff member with existing state assessment responsibilities such as a district or school test coordinator?

   3. How much authority is being delegated?

   4. How can school staff obtain clarification of the district's expectations for cooperation in the investigation?

B. Reviewing the state's directive to investigate

   1. What is the state asking for in the way of an investigation and what information is being provided?

   2. If a "tip" was received by the state or a central school district office, what was the nature of that tip?

   3. Were specific educators mentioned by name?

   4. Is the problem described as occurring on one specific testing occasion or is the charge that there has been pervasive misbehavior?

   5. What exactly is the state asking to receive from the district as a result of the investigation?

C. Reviewing available information

   1. How much detail has the state or a tipster provided about testing anomalies?

   2. Have unusual test results been identified?

   3. If so, for which grades, subjects, and classes?

   4. Are comparison data being provided that help characterize the "unusualness" of particular testing outcomes?

   5. Can the district use its own data sets to evaluate the unusualness of particular test results?

D. Planning and conducting interviews

1. For individuals who are called upon to conduct interviews, how will they be trained for that purpose?

2. How will the DOE ensure that they understand the requirements of the state, any school district rules that apply, and the general context for protecting the rights of all involved in investigations?

3. What are the particular forms to be used and the procedures for requesting interviews and recording results?

4. Can a student, teacher, or administrator who is to be interviewed have someone accompany them during an interview such as an attorney or a union representative?

5. Who will have access to the results of the interviews and on what schedule?

E. Preparing interview questions – The following are questions of the type that warrant consideration when developing an interview guide for investigations.

1. Were you provided with security training? When and by whom?

2. When did testing materials arrive at a school? In the case of computer-based testing (CBT), when did you first have access to the examination questions?

3. Where were physical test materials stored?

4. Who had access to the test materials in both paper and pencil (P&P) and CBT delivered exams?

5. Describe the process on test day for the school as a whole and for each testing room.

6. How were test materials collected and mailed from the school when testing was complete?

7. Did you observe any testing irregularities in your school on any of the testing days?

8. Are there ways that you would like to see test security practices enhanced?

F. Developing a report

1. What information in the report needs to be explicit about the evidence that is being sought and the level of detail needed?

2. Is it sufficient to note that staff received training in test administration techniques at district and school test coordinator sessions or are specific details required?

3. What are the key findings in the report that need to be highlighted and provided if the investigation uncovered security shortcomings?

APPENDIX G. *Testing and Data Integrity in the Administration of Statewide Student Assessment Programs* (NCME, 2012)

2424 American Lane • Madison, WI 53704-3102 USA
Phone: 1-608-443-2487 • Fax: 1-608-443-2474 • Website: www.ncme.org

November 27, 2012

Dear Colleagues:

It is a time of great promise in large-scale assessment. However, with the increasing reliance on test scores to inform important educational decisions has come increasing reports of inappropriate behavior. On statewide student achievement tests, this has occurred both on the part of students who take those tests, and of educators and other adults charged with administering them and protecting the integrity of the results. To be useful for educational decision making, the data from tests must be protected from threats to validity such as cheating in its many forms.

Statewide assessment programs make sizeable investments in test development, administration, and scoring activities. In contrast, comparatively few resources are typically allocated to assuring the integrity of test data, and few guidelines have existed to aid those who assumed those obligations.

Thus, as President of the National Council on Measurement in Education (NCME), I asked the association's Test Score Integrity Work Group to take on the task of developing user-friendly, technically-sound guidelines for promoting the integrity of test data. The mission of NCME is clear: To advance the science and practice of measurement in education. As the leading professional association of testing specialists, NCME members possessed the knowledge, experience, and expertise to assume such a task. The Work Group was requested to produce a set of clear, non-technical guidelines that would be useful and broadly accessible to educators, policy makers, legislators, test developers, and the public.

The attached document, *Testing and Data Integrity in the Administration of Statewide Student Assessment Programs*, is the culmination of the Work Group's efforts. The group brought keen insights, broad input, deep experience, diverse perspectives, and technical accuracy to bear in a way that has resulted in a brief, concrete, and comprehensive document that advances the practice of large-scale student assessment.

I believe you will find the document useful, and I hope that you will join me in commending the Work Group for their contribution. We, the members of NCME, welcome your comments and suggestions as we work together toward the common goals of improving assessment and increasing achievement for all students.

Sincerely,

Gregory J. Cizek, PhD
President, National Council on Measurement in Education

Gregory Cizek   President
Wim van der Linden   Vice-President
Linda Cook   Past President

TESTING AND DATA INTEGRITY IN THE ADMINISTRATION OF STATEWIDE STUDENT ASSESSMENT PROGRAMS

October, 2012

Contributors to this document, listed alphabetically, include N. Scott Bishop (ACT, Inc.), Kristen Huff (USNY Regents Research Fund), Karen Mitchell (Association of Medical Colleges), Sherry Rose-Bond (Columbus City Schools, Columbus, OH), Paul Stemmer (Michigan Department of Education), E. Roger Trent (Consultant, Columbus, OH), and James Wollack (University of Wisconsin). We are grateful to all of the National Council on Measurement in Education members who took the time to comment on an earlier version of this document.

The NCME mission is to advance the science and practice of measurement in education.

Goals of the organization include:

1. Encourage scholarly development in educational measurement

    a. Improve measurement instruments and procedures for their administration, scoring, interpretation, and use

    b. Improve applications of measurement in assessment of individuals, groups, and evaluation of educational programs

2. Disseminate knowledge about educational measurement, including

    a. Theory, techniques, and instrumentation for the measurement of educationally relevant human, institutional and social characteristics

    b. Procedures appropriate to the interpretation and use of such techniques and instruments

    c. Applications of educational measurement with individuals and groups

3. Increase NCME's influence within the educational measurement community to ensure sound and ethical measurement practices

4. Influence public policy and practice concerning educational measurement

5. Promote awareness of measurement in education as a field of study and work to encourage entry into the field and interdisciplinary collaboration

6. Provide members with a strong professional identity and intellectual home in educational measurement and enhance the value of membership in NCME

7. Increase the operating and financial capacity of the association to enhance its effectiveness and its national recognition

Copyright ©2012 by the National Council on Measurement in Education. All rights reserved.

TESTING AND DATA INTEGRITY IN THE ADMINISTRATION OF STATEWIDE STUDENT ASSESSMENT PROGRAMS

Testing and data integrity on statewide assessments is defined as the establishment of a comprehensive set of policies and procedures for: a) the proper preparation of students, b) the management and administration of the test(s) that will lead to accurate and appropriate reporting of assessment results, and c) maintaining the security of assessment materials for future use. The policies must ensure that all students have had equal opportunities to show their knowledge, skills, and abilities and have been actively involved in demonstrating those opportunities through their engagement with the test. Educators, students, parents, school boards, legislators, researchers, and the public must have confidence that psychometrically-sound testing, scoring, and reporting will be handled ethically and in accordance with the best administrative practices to ensure that results accurately reflect *each student's own true educational knowledge, skills, and abilities*. For purposes of this document, we focus on the aspects of *test data integrity* that relate to maintaining test security and safeguarding against artificially inflated scores.

WHY TEST DATA INTEGRITY IS IMPORTANT

Federal[1], state, and local education decisions are based on results of statewide assessments. Assessment requires that results be: accurate, fair, useful, interpretable, and comparable. The technical merits of test scores must meet professional and industry standards with respect to fairness, reliability, and validity. Test data must be free from the effects of cheating **and** security breaches and represent the true achievement measures of students who are sufficiently and appropriately engaged in the test administration. Cheating, falsifying data, security breaches, and other actions of academic fraud compromise the standards of fairness, reliability, and validity by polluting data. When cheating occurs, the public loses confidence in the testing program and in the educational system which may have serious educational, fiscal, and political consequences. Policies and procedures must ensure that all students have appropriate, fair, and equal opportunities to show their knowledge, skills, and abilities. Students who need accommodations due to language differences or students with disabilities may require appropriate modifications to materials and administrative procedures to ensure fair access to the assessment of their skills.

WHO IS RESPONSIBLE FOR TEST DATA INTEGRITY?

Test data integrity is a shared responsibility among all educators, test professionals, and students[2]. The ultimate leadership for ensuring data integrity belongs to State Educational Agencies (SEAs). However, Local Educational Agencies (LEAs) staff and students are critical partners in ensuring established test policies and procedures are properly implemented and followed. Assessment consortia, test publishers, and contractors also play a significant role. SEAs must have appropriate policies and legislation that address these issues, including descriptions of requirements, expectations, and consequences for assessment activities. LEA policies and procedures must address how data integrity is ensured within each district and school.

---

1   The U.S. Education Department (ED) sets policy for score use in federal programs. ED can help ensure that legislation and rules governing test security are established by states and that there is appropriate consistency across entities. ED might also consider establishment of a repository for policies, rules and best practices that will help SEAs and LEAs ensure data integrity.

2   For an example of ethical standards, see NCME's *Code of Professional Responsibilities in Educational Measurement* at the following link: http://www.ncme.org/resources/code.cfm

RECOMMENDED PRACTICES

1. Entities should develop a comprehensive data integrity policy to ensure the fairness, reliability, validity, and comparability of results when tests and results are used as intended[3]. The policy should define assessment integrity (and why it is important) and set forth standardized practices that are practical within typical school environments, resources, and operations. It should define proper and prohibited conduct and include how to prevent irregularities. It should establish required security guidelines for protecting test materials from security breaches (where students who have not taken the test would get access to questions) and preserve questions for future use. School personnel should provide input during policy development and be given ample lead time for implementation before any new policy becomes effective.

Implementation plans should be tailored to the purpose of testing, how test scores will be used, and the format of test administration[4]. The policy should describe specific, required security measures, testing procedures, and testing conditions. Clear and consistent written procedures should describe preventive actions, appropriate and inappropriate actions, communication plans, and remediation steps.

The following points should be covered in the policy[5]: staff training and professional development, maintaining security of materials and other prevention activities, appropriate and inappropriate test preparation and test administration activities, data collection and forensic analyses, incident reporting, investigation, enforcement, and consequences. Further, the policy should document the staff authorized to respond to questions about the policy and outline the roles and responsibilities of individuals if a test security breach arises. The policy should also have a communication and remediation response plan in place (if, when, how, who) for contacting impacted parties, correcting the problem and communicating with media in a transparent manner.

2. Assessment Consortia, State Educational Agencies (SEA) and Local Educational Agencies (LEA), including school districts, and building administrative staff, should develop and implement appropriate training in proper administrative procedures and methods to prevent test irregularities. Training should provide an overview of ethical and proper administration procedures and stress the importance of academic and assessment integrity as a means of avoiding serious negative consequences for the testing program and its potential damage to the educational reputation of students and schools. Staff and students should understand and support monitoring efforts to report and detect breaches of security, cheating, and other improper behavior.

Training materials should address the difference in secure and non-secure testing materials (e.g., released materials, practice materials, etc.) and provide clear examples of what behavior is unacceptable during and after testing[6].

3　SEAs, LEAs, and schools must disseminate this information to all staff who participate in testing. Roles and responsibilities should be aligned (i.e., the SEA's plan will drive the LEA responsibilities, and in turn, the LEA's plan will drive the school's).

4　Threats for an end-of-course computerized test are different than those for a paper-and-pencil test used for accountability. Testing practices change (e.g., pencil and paper tests may become computerized), so data integrity plans will need to be updated accordingly.

5　More information and resources that may be helpful for developing these policies are provided in the Appendices. Consider utilizing technical advisors (e.g., SEA technical advisory groups) to vet the plans. Peer review processes might also be considered.

6　See Appendix A for some examples.

Finally, training should ensure that staff and students are aware of the consequences if they are found to have engaged in conduct that threatens the integrity of test administration and results. Procedures to be followed in the event of a staff member or student being accused of misconduct should be articulated and reviewed in training. The procedures should address the appropriate understanding and compliance with nondisclosure and confidentiality agreements, as well as participation forms for verifying that staff have participated in training. The expectation of compliance with administration standards should also be made clear to students. Older students might be asked to sign assessment conduct and responsibility statements as well.

3. Entities should engage in proactive prevention to minimize threats to data integrity. One source of cheating by staff is lack of understanding about what are acceptable and unacceptable behaviors and the important reasons behind the need for accurate test results. Efforts should be taken to eliminate opportunities for test takers to attain scores by fraudulent means, or opportunities for school staff or other stakeholders to tamper (violate instructions for appropriate administration or accommodations) with computer-based testing systems, paper-based test booklets, answer documents and other secure materials and information. Monitoring programs where operational assessments are observed by SEA agents also helps ensure assessment integrity[7]. Results of monitoring should be used for prevention and training (feedback to the school) as well as to identify potential irregularities.

Students should be told about the importance of the assessments and why it is important that the scores reflect their true abilities.

4. Entities should ensure that all test administrations follow standardized procedures as appropriate to the student (e.g., some students may require accommodations) and in accordance with the Standards for Educational and Psychological Testing (1999) or any of its subsequent revisions. Any and all guidelines regarding materials prohibited in testing areas should be followed[8].

5. A clear and fair monitoring and investigation process to identify irregularities must be established by the SEA and a local version by each LEA. Entities should ensure all evidence of irregularities that are collected are comprehensive and facilitate subsequent analyses. This should include a detailed record of test administrators, support staff (proctors), and teachers' names. The requirements for data files used for integrity analysis will likely evolve as analytic techniques evolve[9]. In documenting irregularities, collection of physical evidence (e.g., cheat sheets), photographic evidence (e.g., notes written on arm, desk, etc.), examinee handwriting in test booklets or scratch paper, and other specific observational notes can play an important role during follow-up investigations.

For computer-based testing, Internet activities should be monitored and logged (sites visited, screenshots taken, etc.) for all persons who access school and district servers and the activities of all users of school/district computers. Computers should be checked for prohibited software and malicious programs.

7 Other preventative suggestions are provided in Appendix B.

8 See Appendix C for some examples of materials students have used to gain unfair advantage over others.

9 See Appendix D.

6. Entities (e.g., SEAs or their designees) should conduct comprehensive integrity analyses at multiple levels (e.g., district, school, classroom, and/or students) for all large-scale programs where consequences for students and/or school personnel are present. State results typically provide the best comparison for evaluating schools and districts. Such analyses and reports should be reviewed by the SEA's technical advisory panel. The analyses should include multiple methods and follow best practices to ensure the highest likelihood of detecting misconduct, while using appropriate statistical controls to minimize false detections. Results should only identify students, classes, schools, and districts where there is strong evidence that further investigation for possible improprieties is warranted. Investigations and subsequent actions should focus on appropriate remediation and future prevention of any irregularities discovered.

7. In the interest of protecting the privacy of both those being investigated for potential cheating and those contributing information to the investigation, entities should ensure that reports of suspected cheating, security breaches, as well as other suspicious activities are developed following clear and transparent guidelines, and in accordance with the Freedom of Information Act, Family Educational Rights and Privacy Act and other applicable laws or professional guidelines. Individuals who report suspected violations must be protected from retribution. Multiple reporting avenues (e.g., 800 numbers, e-mail, web forms, etc.) should be provided. Clear methods, procedures, data analysis and findings and reports should be thoroughly documented. A secure database collections system for capturing reported incidents should be created and maintained. Appropriate sections of the system should be made accessible to all LEAs.

8. Entities should ensure the appropriate investigation of any reported incidents and irregularities that are flagged during forensics analysis. Qualified and trained staff responsible for investigating violations should be identified in advance. The SEA should develop policies for when and how to turn investigations over to a third party so as to avoid potential conflicts of interest. Investigations should occur in a timely fashion and written reports should be given to the SEA along with remediation plans for any problem areas.

9. SEAs and LEAs must develop plans to address breaches of assessment integrity and to handle the consequences in a fair and appropriate manner and most importantly, to ensure that the offense does not happen in the future. Sanctions or remediation must be proportional relative to the offense and equivalent to other policies. All parties should create and maintain due process and appeal procedures for suspect students and staff. The accused should be informed of the allegations or complaints and the circumstances behind them (statistical detection, reported violation, etc.).

10. As testing technology evolves, security needs and how we define test and data integrity must keep pace. Policies and procedures should be reviewed to ensure compliance with the principles of assessment integrity. Computer-based testing will present different challenges based on the hardware (mobile vs. desktop configurations), the software, and Internet configurations (network security, social media, etc.). A few examples include greater accessibility to biometric identification procedures, built-in universal design, handwriting analysis, time-stamping items and events, video/audio monitoring systems, and improved real-time and post-hoc statistical anomaly detection techniques.

APPENDIX A: SOME THREATS TO TEST INTEGRITY

The following is a non-exhaustive list of examples which have the potential to artificially inflate test scores.

Before Testing

- Using actual or live test items in continuous drilling instead of focusing on assessing the underlying learning standards
- Using secure/unreleased items to train students that violates the administration manual guidelines
- Previewing the test before administration
- Excluding selected students from the administration (e.g., not allowing lower-achieving students to sit for an exam in order to raise group averages)
- Using unauthorized test preparation materials
- Failure to store secure test materials
- Improper or ineffective test administration training practices (failure to train staff, failure to devise effective practices)

During Testing

- Students copying answers from other students
- Students providing assistance to or accepting assistance from other students
- Students or teachers using prearranged signals (e.g., tapping, signing, voice inflection, facial expression) to provide correct answers to students
- Failing to follow prescribed test administration procedures leading to administration irregularities, e.g., incomplete student responses, or providing too much information so as to assist the students in correctly answering questions
- Inappropriate proctoring by coaching or signaling students (e.g., hints, rephrasing questions, voice or facial inflection), pointing out errors, or otherwise identifying correct answers during the exam
- Displaying improper information in student assessment rooms
    - Putting up posters or other materials that provide test answers
    - Failing to cover existing information boards, posters
- Giving unauthorized students extended time, prohibited materials, or other non-standard conditions.
- Allowing unauthorized people in the testing area (e.g., media, other students, teachers, or parents)
- Inappropriate or over-accommodated student accommodation practices

After Testing

- Altering student answer documents, changing answers, or filling in omitted items
- Falsifying identification or demographic information for students
- Exposing or releasing items that will appear on future test forms
- Divulging details about test items to others who have yet to test (note: school staff should explicitly instruct students not to do this)
- For performance-based assessments, allowing local scoring that may favor responses of local students or staff scoring their own students
- During reporting, inaccurately summarizing or interpreting test results to the students' advantage
- Not returning all secure testing material
- Photocopying, reproducing, disclosing, or disseminating testing materials in any way
- Failing to submit answer sheets for students expected to do poorly
- Any other action resulting in data that misrepresents the achievement levels of students within classes, schools, districts, and states

APPENDIX B: SOME PREVENTIVE ACTIONS

The following is a non-exhaustive list of examples.

PAPER-AND-PENCIL ADMINISTRATION

Security of Materials

- Keep sensitive test materials (live test items and booklets, computer screens, or computer testing access, etc.) secure and accounted for at all times (before, during, and after testing)
  - Have a dedicated, secure place to store materials that prevents non-authorized access to test material
  - Determine which staffers have legitimate access to the storage area
  - If the storage area cannot be completely sequestered, track all staff who enter/exit the area
- Determine which staffers are responsible for maintaining the chain of custody over test materials (this applies to all administrative staff who handle test and proctoring materials)
- Pre-seal booklets (sometimes cost-prohibitive) or provide self-seals for students' test documents

Distribution and Collection of Materials

- Schedule the times that materials will be distributed and collected
- Specify and document check in/check out procedures for materials
- Promulgate a list of detailed procedures for reporting missing and damaged test materials

Test Administration

- Use seating charts and assign seating, as appropriate
- Require appropriate identification or recognition of each student as appropriate
- Seat students an appropriate distance apart
- Restrict or prohibit (as your administration manual requires) mobile cameras, cell phones, and other similar devices
- Use only trained test proctors and provide proper supervision (use proctor guidelines)
- Establish qualifications requirements (i.e., education and credential) for proctors and test
- administrators
- Have rooms proctored during the entire administration
- Document proctor names and locations of the assessment
- Independently monitor test administrations on a random basis
- Test all eligible students
- Do not allow teachers to test their own students unless necessary or allowed for by required accommodations
- Maintain established security procedures throughout make-up testing and special accommodations
- Establish common scheduling time and calendar for testing
- Have materials returned immediately after testing
- Test all examinees in a narrow testing window, scheduling primary subject matter tests on the same day and at the same time to reduce possible collusion and mitigate damages from a security breach
- Clearly identify prohibited behavior and items as well as rules for handling irregularities

COMPUTER-BASED ADMINISTRATION

Security of Materials

- Keep screens out of view of each student or others (position monitors, cardboard screens, and carrels strategically)

- Establish a building testing schedule so all students are tested in the same subject before beginning the next subject

- Time-stamp all student and staff access

- Specify disallowed access times (i.e., weekends, holidays, after hours, etc.)

- Ensure that students are locked out from accessing unauthorized computer applications, including the use of the Internet, during assessment

- Lock-out access to the test after testing windows are completed

- Prohibit students from accessing memory storage or Wi-Fi on mobile devices

APPENDIX C: SOME MATERIALS ALLOWED AND PROHIBITED DURING EXAMS

The following is a non-exhaustive list of examples. Always consult your specific administration manual.

Items Frequently Allowed in Testing Areas

- Admission ticket
- School-issued ID
- Government-issued photo ID
- Number two pencils (wooden)
- Quality erasers
- Highlighters, other approved writing implements
- Silent or beeping timers
- Foam ear plugs or other noise-blocking devices
- Transparent containers (e.g., "Ziploc bags")
- Approved calculators
- Water bottles, as approved
- Dictionaries, as approved

Items Frequently Prohibited in Testing Areas

- All electronic devices used for communication or data storage (e.g., cell phones, book readers, tablets, pagers, cameras, non-approved calculators, music players, voice recorders, etc.)
- Study, review, or other information resource materials (dictionaries, thesauruses, encyclopedias,
- spelling and grammar checkers)
- Correction fluid, correction pens
- Large rubber bands, large pencil erasers
- Boxes, pencil cases, eyeglass cases, or other opaque containers
- Briefcases, backpacks, purses
- Clothing that could be disruptive or present a potential test or student security threat (e.g., hats, scarves, hoodies, loose or bulky clothing)
- Earphones, headphones, ear buds unless as a required accommodation or computer administration requirement
- Mechanical pencils or ink pens (except for notes for computer-based testing or other exceptions)
- Smoking materials, food, beverages (Note: case-by-case exceptions for medical reasons can be made)

APPENDIX D: DATA COLLECTION AND ANALYSIS

Forensics should be considered carefully and determined as appropriate for each test by Technical Advisory consults and/or committees. Analysis should be technically sound and carefully targeted to avoid false positives, while simultaneously maximizing true positives. Suggestions of what to collect and look for include the following:

Suggestions for Data Collection

- Capture both teacher and proctor names (e.g., on classroom 'header' sheets) and include this info in data files for potential use in forensic analyses
- Expand the contents of the data file(s) used for integrity analysis by including:
  - actual student scan/scored vectors (e.g., A, B, C, D for 'wrongs,' 1, 2, 3, 4 for 'rights')
  - ability information (raw and/or scaled scores)
  - pre-erasure answer strings
  - post-erasure answer strings
  - string of erasure types (wrong-to-right, wrong-to-wrong, right-to-wrong, no erasure)
  - darkness gradient for post-erasure item responses
  - pixel coverage of post-erasure item responses

Suggestions for Forensics Analysis

- Suspicious changes in test scores in adjoining test years
- Suspicious changes in student demographics across years
- Suspicious erasures
  - high erasure rates and, in particular, high wrong-to-right erasures
  - erasures with different darkness and pixel coverage than non-erased responses.
  - contrast erasure rates for pilot versus operational items
  - consistency of erasures (i.e., erasures on the same set of items) for students within classrooms, schools, and districts versus the state
- Speed of responding on computer-based tests
- Similar answer patterns between pairs or groups of students
- Similar items being flagged as erased between groups of students
- Similar responses to open-ended items
- Inconsistent item responses pattern—response aberrations, in particular for pre- and post-erasure responses
- Outliers in scatter plots of subject area scores (e.g., what classes had mathematics scores that were outliers based on reading score performance)
- Prior test administration common items (e.g., one year back) vs. common items from several years prior (multiple years back) as well as comparison between operational and pilot sections may help identify students who had pre-knowledge of questions
- Comparisons between summative assessments and earlier formative/interim assessments, third party assessments, such as NAEP, or other academic efforts (GPA, class rank, coursework)

APPENDIX E: RESOURCES

Policies and procedures must be based on best practices in testing. Some of these documents are showing their age and are in various stages of revision. Among the documents to be considered in establishing the definitions and descriptions of best practices are:

American Federation of Teachers, National Council on Measurement in Education, & National Education Association. (1990). *Standards for Teacher Competence in Educational Assessment of Students*. Washington, DC: NCME.

American Educational Research Association, American Psychological Association, & National Council on Measurement in Education (1999). *Standards for Educational and Psychological Testing*. Washington, DC: AERA.

National Council on Measurement in Education (1995). *Code of Professional Responsibilities in Educational Measurement*. Washington, DC: Author.

Joint Committee on Testing Practices (2004). *Code of Fair Testing Practices in Education*. Washington, DC: American Psychological Association.

Council of Chief State School Officers and the Association of Test Publishers (2010). Operational Best Practices for Statewide Large-Scale Assessment Programs. Washington, DC.

APPENDIX H. *State and District-level Academic Dishonesty Policies* (Hanover Research, 2012)

[Authors' note: only the title page and Introduction to this report are provided here. The full report may be requested by contacting Dr. John Olson at jmclkolson@yahoo.com.]

Title page

State- and District-Level Academic Dishonesty Policies

Prepared for the Council of Chief School State Officers

In this report, Hanover Research presents an overview of state- and district-level policies regarding academic dishonesty.

HANOVER RESEARCH APRIL 2012

© 2012 Hanover Research – District Administration Practice

Introduction

The issue of cheating is attracting increasing attention in the United States. Scandals involving teacher misconduct – ranging from teachers preparing students for state assessment tests with actual test questions,[1,2] to teachers assisting students as they take standardized tests,[3] to teachers providing students with extra time on standardized tests,[4] to teachers correcting students' completed standardized tests[5] – have erupted from Pennsylvania to California. In a recent survey of 40,000 American youth conducted by the Josephson Institute's Center for Youth Ethics, "a majority of students (59 percent) admitted cheating on a test during the last year, with 34 percent doing it more than two times. One in three admitted they used the Internet to plagiarize an assignment."[6] In a dramatic instance of what unfortunately may be a trend, 20 students were recently charged with "accepting payment or paying others to take the SAT and ACT between 2008 and 2011."[7] The principal of the New York school at the center of this scandal warns that his school is not an exception.

1 Blume, Howard. "L.A. school board to close six charter schools caught cheating." March 02, 2011. *Los Angeles Times*. http://articles.latimes.com/2011/mar/02/local/la-me-0302-lausd-charters-20110302

2 Toppo, Greg, Denise Amos, Jack Gillum, and Jodi Upton. "When test scores seem too good to believe." March 17, 2011. *USA Today*. http://www.usatoday.com/news/education/2011-03-06-school-testing_N.htm

3 DeNardo, Mike. "School District Investigating Cheating Allegations at Hunting Park School." January 14, 2012. CBSPhilly. http://philadelphia.cbslocal.com/2012/02/14/school-district-of-philadelphia-investigating-cheating-allegations-at-cayuga-elementary-school-in-hunting-park/

4 Ibid.

5 Strauss, Valerie. "Shocking Details of Atlanta Cheating Scandal." July 7, 2011. *The Washington Post POSTLOCAL*. http://www.washingtonpost.com/blogs/answer-sheet/post/shocking-details-of-atlanta-cheating-scandal/2011/07/06/gIQAQPhY2H_blog.html

6 "The Ethics of American Youth: 2010" Josephson Institute. 2011. http://charactercounts.org/programs/reportcard/2010/installment02_report-card_honesty-integrity.html

7 Anderson, Jenny; Willie Hu. "20 Students Now Accused in L.I. Case on Cheating." November 22, 2011. *The New York Times*. http://www.nytimes.com/2011/11/23/education/more-students-charged-in-long-island-sat-cheating-case.html?pagewanted=all

8 Lewis, Terry. "Report: 'Disgrace' in county schools (updated with list of teachers)." December 20, 2011. *The Albany Herald*. http://www.albanyherald.com/news/2011/dec/20/governors-crct-report-names-11-dcss-elementary-pri/

9 Strauss, *op. cit*.

Investigations of cheating scandals involving teachers have pointed to pressure to meet Acceptable Yearly Progress standards under No Child Left Behind, fear of being perceived as a failure, failures of leadership and increased emphasis on test scores in teacher evaluations as reasons cheating flourished.[8,9] Among other factors, pressure to excel, the sense that it is cheating is common, and the ease of cheating are cited as reasons students cheat. Preempting cheating requires that strict and clear cheating policies be established at multiple levels of the American educational system.

This report provides an overview of cheating policies established by educational bodies at the state and district level across the United States. To garner information about state policies, Hanover Research contacted representatives at all 51 state departments of education (the 50 states plus the District of Columbia). Fifteen of these fifty-one departments responded with information, for a 29% response rate. In terms of the district-level analysis, Hanover initially planned to review policies for six districts per state—the two largest districts, the two smallest districts, and two districts in the middle. The lack of information for the smallest districts, however, prompted us to revise our approach. We instead opted to profile four districts per state: the two largest districts and two districts with enrollments of approximately 2,000. The final report is comprehensive at the district level and presents significant information at the state level.

The report contains the following four sections:

❖ **Section One: Overview of State-Level Policies**

This section summarizes answers to the five questions we asked each department of education representative about state-level cheating policies.

❖ **Section Two: Overview of District-Level Policies**

This section summarizes the cheating policies of the two largest districts in each state and two districts with enrollments around 2,000 students.

❖ **Appendix A: State Education Department Policy Profiles**

This section reproduces state education department representatives' responses to Hanover Research in full detail.

❖ **Appendix B: District Profiles**

This section presents comprehensive profiles of the cheating policies of each district featured in section two.

Below, we summarize our key findings.

Key Findings: State-Level

❖ **Focus of Cheating Policies**. Cheating policies at the state level are almost exclusively focused on standardized assessment security.

❖ **Responsibility for Establishing Policy on Cheating on State Assessments.** While the majority of respondents indicate that policy regarding cheating on state assessments is made solely at the state level, several respondents indicated that local districts are either allowed or required to make additional district-level policies. A few state department representatives indicated that the department of education tries to work with districts when they construct state policy.

❖ **Responsibility for Investigating Allegations of Cheating on State Assessments.** When cheating allegations are reported or irregularities identified on state assessments, it is most often the responsibility of the school district to investigate and report on progress and discoveries. A constitutional or legal commitment to local control is most often cited as the reason for this delegation, though some departments indicate that it reflects a common belief that districts can more effectively address local problems. While the district investigates, the state department primarily provides guidelines, reviews reports, and invalidates impacted test scores. Wisconsin stands out as an exception; its Department of Public Instruction is particularly active in investigating allegations.

Key Findings: District-Level

❖ **Student-focused Academic Dishonesty Policy.** Policies on student academic dishonesty are by no means universal at the district level: at least one and often two districts of the four we profiled per state made no reference to cheating in the sources we reviewed. The cheating policies we did find at the district level most often include calls for students to act "with integrity" and admonitions against using electronic communication devices to plagiarize. Consequences are often either applicable to a range of offenses or not addressed at all; cited consequences include a zero on the related assignment, counseling, teacher-parent conferences, the revoking of privileges (for instance, one can no longer be named "valedictorian"), suspension, and expulsion.

❖ **Teacher-focused Academic Dishonesty Policy.** District-level "dishonesty" policies that do reference teachers seldom address cheating, rather focusing on honesty or integrity in general. This injunction is sometimes found in Board of Education policy manuals or student handbooks with no other information about cheating policies. The Cedar Rapids Community School District in Iowa is an exception to the lack of explicit policies at the district level concerning academic dishonesty as it relates to teachers. It has an explicit policy regarding administrator-related cheating on standardized assessments.

❖ **Priority Given to Cheating Policy.** Policies are frequently buried in various subsections of the district Board of Education Policy rather than placed in more accessible locations like district-wide Student Codes of Conduct or in Student Handbooks. The lack of visibility of these policies suggests that establishing and enforcing policies against student academic dishonesty is not a priority for district-level education administrators.

❖ **The Effect of District Enrollment on Policy.** There are no significant differences in the cheating policies of relatively large and relatively small, except that districts with higher enrollments more often have information available on their websites.

APPENDIX I. Results from Survey of State TILSA Members on Test Security

Results of 2012 Survey of State TILSA SCASS Members on Test Security

Technical Issues in Large-Scale Assessment (TILSA)

State Collaboratives on Assessment and Student Standards (SCASS)

May 2012

Rationale:

The 2012-13 TILSA Test Security Project begins with the researching and gathering of information about current practices, resources, needs, and advice about test security. John Olson (Assessment Solutions Group) and John Fremer (Caveon Test Securities) will work with a TILSA workgroup to produce a Guidebook, entitled, *Preventing, Detecting, and Investigating Test Security Irregularities: A Comprehensive Guidebook on Test Security for States.* As part of the information gathering process, a survey was sent to all TILSA State Members to learn about their current practices, challenges, and needs. Information from this survey will be used to inform work on the Test Security Project.

Methodology:

All TILSA State Members were asked to complete an online survey during the month of April 2012. Of the 24 TILSA State Members, 22 (91.7%) submitted responses. One response was requested for each state, even where there were multiple state TILSA representatives. The survey was designed with skip logic so that which questions were encountered was controlled by responses to previous questions. For that reason, the response count is presented along with the results for each question.

Organization of Results:

Results are presented in four sections:

> Section A: State Test Security Policies and Practices

> Section B: State Test Security Breaches

> Section C: What is Important/Worrisome to States

> Section D: What Should be in the TILSA Test Security Guidebook

A. State Test Security Policies and Practices

1. **Which of the following test security measures are used in your state assessment program?**

		Response Count	Percentage Yes
a.	Formal policies and procedures regarding cheating	22	**90.9**
b.	A written test security plan	21	66.7
c.	Training of state staff on test security procedures	22	90.9
d.	Designation of an individual responsible for test security investigations	22	90.9
e.	Scheduled/required local educator staff training on test security	22	86.4
f.	Defined punishment for those found cheating	22	54.5
g.	A separate test security budget	21	4.8

➢ **Additional Comments**

❖ *Some of the above are in development.*

❖ *Test security is addressed in Rule and in Administration manuals.*

❖ *Mandatory Annual Test Security Agreement signed by LEA Superintendents, Charter Representatives, District Test Coordinators, and Test Administrators.*

❖ *[Our state] is somewhere between yes and no. I have chosen No since our policies and procedures are not as well defined as they should be.*

❖ *Annual ethics training required for administrators and educators involved in test administration.*

❖ *Tests are voided if cheating is determined to occur. Disciplinary action for personnel found cheating is a district decision. A law was passed that protects individuals who report test security breaches.*

❖ *Local test impropriety investigation and reporting to the state. State-level tracking and reporting of test impropriety trends, with refinement of test security policies to address emerging risks.*

❖ *We are in process of improving policies following a Caveon Security Audit.*

2. **A Test Security Kit may provide instructions about a state's security-related procedures, processes, and regulations, including the escalation path to be followed in the event of a test security breach. Does your state provide any kind of Test Security Kit for schools?**

	Response Count	Percentage Yes
	22	**40.9**

➢ **Additional Comments**

❖ *Our state is in the process of developing a test security kit, beyond that of required sign-off forms.*

❖ *Kit information described above would be found in Test Administrator's training manual. Also available in the document Testing Security Protocol and Procedures for School Personnel.*

❖ *We have produced a provisional test security kit this year that is being piloted in several districts.*

❖ *We have an integrity guide that covers a lot of this.*

❖ *This information is disseminated in our Test Examiner's Manual and Test Coordinator's Manual.*

❖ *Part IV - Test Security of the state's test administration manual includes detailed description of test security requirements, examples of improprieties, detailed description of impropriety investigation and reporting requirements, consequences for test improprieties, role-specific security assurance forms, and a test impropriety report form.*

3. **For the last three years, has your state consistently conducted statistical/psychometric analyses of test responses to detect indications of test security concerns on the statewide assessment?**

	Response Count	Percentage **Yes**
	22	27.3

4. **Briefly describe the types of analyses your state performs on test responses.**
   (for the 6 states who responded "Yes" on Question #3)

   ❖ *Erasure*
   ❖ *Erasure analyses (Overall and WTR) controlled for population size, Year-to-year improvement in proficiency, Large clusters of exceedingly high growth (operationalized using student growth percentiles)*
   ❖ *WTR erasures, high growth, within classroom deviation*
   ❖ *Erasure analysis*
   ❖ *Erasure analysis and perfect score check, duplicate names*
   ❖ *Erasure Analysis conducted by vendor (beginning SY 11-12), analyses identifying statistical anomalies of value-added scores conducted by vendor, SAS analyses identifying statistical and practical anomalies of mean scale scores and performance levels*

5. **Briefly describe how you use the results of these analyses.**
   (for the 6 states who responded "Yes" on Question #3)

   ❖ *Notify districts or charters of abnormally high percentages of wrong to right erasures.*
   ❖ *Any one indicator can trigger the state to examining all three quantitative indicators. However, the state uses more than just quantitative indicators. The quantitative data provides an initial examination of whether there appears to be a pervasive and/or severe concern around the validity of data in a given school or under a given test administrator.*
   ❖ *Flag classrooms for further investigation*
   ❖ *Void test results*
   ❖ *Ask district/school to conduct investigation and/or provide explanations*
   ❖ *Analyses are combined to identify possible instances of cheating - consultation with district leaders on next steps occurs*

6. **Does your state have procedures in place for conducting an investigation of a possible test security incident?**

	Response Count	Percentage **Yes**
	22	95.5

7. **Which best describes the role of school district personnel in test security investigations in your state?**
   Response Count = 21

		Percentage
a.	District personnel conduct the investigation.	61.9
b.	District personnel facilitate the investigation which is conducted by others.	4.8
c.	District personnel are typically the target of the investigation.	0.0

> **Other Roles of School District Personnel (specified in Question # 7)**

- ❖ *District personnel may conduct an investigation before turning evidence into the [Department], which also conducts an investigation into the alleged test security breach.*
- ❖ *State personnel, in conjunction with district personnel, initiate the investigation. In some cases the state personnel, with the assistance of an investigator from the state's Office of Legal Services (former police officer) take the lead on the investigation.*
- ❖ *Third party*
- ❖ *Depending upon the severity of the case involved, the investigation may be conducted by the SEA or district personnel.*
- ❖ *Typically they provide the tip*
- ❖ *All three of these statements are true, but considerations for test security investigations are done on a case by case basis.*
- ❖ *DOE requires that district personnel conduct first phase of investigation and report findings. DOE then reviews and determines the need to do onsite interviews and further investigation before issuing a report of findings and action, if necessary.*

8. **Briefly describe how investigations are handled in your state.**
   Response Count = 20

- ❖ *Initially, the district conducts the evaluation and submits a report to the state. Further action is dependent upon review of the district report.*
- ❖ *LEAs conduct investigation and present evidence to the state. State then meets in committee and recommends course of action - recommendation provided to SBE if applicable*
- ❖ *The agency receives information on a security issue. The agency contacts the district and asks the district to conduct an investigation and send in a narrative report of the findings. The agency reviews the report and determines if scores need to be suppressed. Agency staff determines if teacher certification should receive the report for possible action against educators involved in the incident.*
- ❖ *Website allows for input of testing allegations. Also, another state agency has 800 number for reporting allegations. Once reported, Dept of Ed staff member conducts investigation.*
- ❖ *All allegations are sent to the Director of Assessment who decides if the allegation is an irregularity or an ethics violation. If it rises to the level of an ethics violation, it is sent to the Professional Licensure Standards Board (PLSB) for processing, investigation, and final disposition. Irregularities are handled in the Office of Student Assessment based on their nature and severity.*
- ❖ *Typically, the flow of behaviors : 1) A written or oral report is received by the building level assessment coordinator 2) Appropriate district personnel are notified 3) Appropriate leadership are notified at district level and contacts the state 4) Investigation team, including district personnel, discuss the allegation tracks the incident 5) State investigative team reviews statements and documents to determine the level of violation, if any 6) State specifies a course of action as defined in state policy*
- ❖ *By a third party but managed by the state*

- ❖ *During testing, I handle all issues with school and district personnel. After testing is over, all issues are reported to the Superintendent who is asked to investigate and report back to the Department within 30 days.*
- ❖ *See page 55 on this document which outlines the process: http://www.mde.k12.ms.us/accred/ Final_2010_11-30-10_manual.pdf*
- ❖ *LEA Assessment Director investigates allegations. Allegations are forwarded to state professional practices advisory commission if appropriate (educator licensing review).*
- ❖ *An initial investigation is conducted at the local level and then reported to the state level if concerns are substantiated. At that point, a formal state level investigation begins with findings presented to the SBE for license and/or score revocation if deemed applicable.*
- ❖ *District Assessment Coordinators conduct investigations. Sometimes they work with HR or other units. The state and district collaborate throughout the investigation.*

❖ The District Test Coordinator or other personnel assigned by the district superintendent conducts the investigation and reports back to the Department of Education. Districts submit a plan of corrective action. Districts may terminate teachers.

❖ Our integrity coordinator is involved and carries out the investigations.

❖ When the state has reasonable evidence to indicate possible cheating, the state informs the district to conduct investigation and provide the state its findings. The state then determines what actions to take based on the findings.

❖ When an irregularity is reported by the public, an anonymous reporter, a school district, a school district employee, or found during a Quality Assurance visit, the report is noted and recorded. The superintendent or assistant superintendent is notified of the report and asked to conduct an investigation, or the Department's area supervisor leads the inquiry into the issue. A response consisting of the findings, corrective/disciplinary actions, and preventative steps is due to the Department within 30 days. All quality assurance issues are reviewed by the Department to determine if any of the cases warrant voiding any scores for accountability. In some cases of testing irregularities, teachers have been disciplined and lost their jobs. In other cases, schools provide additional training and oversight to ensure educators are familiar with all testing requirements. Irregularities include a wide range of issues from schools not locking up testing materials and teachers not timing the tests correctly to teachers reading test questions and helping students with test questions. The testing irregularities reported previously have no geographic or size pattern; reports were received from urban, suburban and rural districts around the state. The Department reviews all reports of irregularity issues and determines if the scores possibly influenced by the irregularity should be voided.

❖ Low level cases are handled by district administrators. Mid-level cases additionally involve state assessment staff persons. High level cases may also include outside investigators.

❖ A school must call or email the state level assessment director to report the key information for a testing incident. The principal at the school and the complex area superintendent are informed about the action that will be taken regarding the student's score for the affected assessment. Any personnel action is handled by the principal in consultation with the state level personnel. Investigations may involve interviews, review of reports, and examination of data.

❖ As a local control state, the investigation of potential test improprieties is conducted at the LEA level. Within each LEA, the district test coordinator is responsible for investigating each potential impropriety to determine what happened and which students' tests were impacted. Depending on the nature of the potential impropriety, the investigation may involve interviews with staff and students. The district test coordinator is then required to submit a formal test impropriety report form to [The Department]. This report includes information about the location where the impropriety occurred, the test subject and grade, a description of the incident, and information identifying each impacted student test. In our state, individual student tests are identified by both a secure student identifier and a result ID; this result ID is a unique ID assigned to each online test opportunity as soon as the opportunity is started. In addition, the report identifies the district's follow-up action (e.g., retraining of staff, implementation of additional security protocols) and the recommended state-level outcome (e.g., whether tests need to be invalidated). Typical improprieties are investigated and reported within the 1-day reporting period. However, for more complex improprieties, [The Department] allows districts up to 30 days from the initial report to complete their full investigation and submit their final report. Upon receipt of the district's report, [The Department] reviews the report for sufficiency and follows up with the district for clarification if it appears that the initial investigation was incomplete or that the district has not taken appropriate follow-up action. Once the investigation is complete, [The Department] then sends the district a letter of final determination documenting the district's investigation and conclusion and confirming the state-determined outcome.

9. **How often does your state conduct routine Internet searches for disclosed content from the statewide assessment?**
Response Count = 22

Percentage

		Percentage
a.	At least once a year	31.8
b.	Every few years	0.0
c.	Never	68.2

10 **In the past three years, how has the amount of time spent on test security in your state changed?**
Response Count = 22

Percentage

		Percentage
a.	The time has increased.	68.2
b.	The time has remained steady.	31.8
c.	The time has decreased.	0.0

B. State Test Security Breaches

While language may be used differently from state to state, for purposes of this survey, TEST SECURITY BREACH is defined as one of the following:

(1) an event, intentional or not, that results in the inappropriate exposure of test items or answers that could potentially impact the accuracy of the test results; OR

(2) an action by others before, during or after a test administration to impact student test scores (e.g., educators changing student answer sheets).

11. In the past three years, have there been any test security breaches in your state assessment program?	Response Count	Percentage Yes
	22	95.5

(Note that the remaining questions in this section were asked only of the 21 states who reported that they have had test security breaches.)

12. Which of the following types of test security breaches have occurred in your state assessment program in the past three years?	Response Count	Percentage Yes
a. Lost or stolen booklets	20	75.0
b. Teachers coaching students before tests on specific questions	20	75.0
c. Teachers providing answers to students during testing	21	85.7
d. Teachers changing student responses after testing	18	61.1
e. Administrators changing student responses after testing	19	52.6
f. Students working together on the test in violation of testing rules	17	35.3
g. Students using technology (e.g., cell phones, PDAs) for cheating	18	50.0
h. Early test takers providing test questions and/or answers to later test takers	18	27.8
i. Test questions and/or answers being posted electronically	19	47.4

➢ **Other Types of Test Security Breaches (specified in Question # 12)**

❖ *I have chosen to answer yes to the issues I remember being reported to me. I suspect that all variations have occurred.*

❖ *Allegations of the above have been reported*

❖ *We have had instances of unintentional disclosure of writing prompt topics and answers as a result of casual family discussions about testing. Some test materials have been pre-viewed, copied and turned into elements of instructional content.*

❖ *The above responses are based on reported allegations.*

❖ *Students accessing non-allowable resources (e.g., notes or textbooks), tests administered by a non-trained test administrator or in a non-secure environment, test administrators incorrectly administering the read-aloud accommodation*

13	In the past three years, has there been a change in the types of test security breaches that have occurred in your state assessment program?	Response Count	Percentage **Yes**
		21	38.1

14	In the past three years, has your state found firm evidence of any teachers or school administrators cheating on behalf of their students?	Response Count	Percentage **Yes**
		21	100.0

15.	In the past three years, which of the following sanctions has your state imposed on a teacher or school administrator for a test security violation?	Response Count	Percentage **Yes**
a.	A stern warning	17	82.4
b.	Transfer from position	16	37.5
c.	Suspension from position	16	56.3
d.	Termination from position	16	50.0
e.	Revocation of certification	15	26.7

➢ **Additional Comments**

❖ *Local districts and school boards have terminated people for testing violations/improprieties.*

❖ *A charter school is having its charter revoked by the state charter board because its director was found to have demanded that his teachers help their students cheat.*

❖ *We have no authority over personnel decisions.*

❖ *I don't know. I deal with the test issues. The district deals with personnel issues, and often the district deals with state over these issues... but I am not privy to the decisions.*

❖ *Explanation: Under the idea of local control, sanctions had been left to the districts, but the state is beginning to take a more active role in this.*

❖ *The Department of Education may only void test scores. The school districts may transfer, write letters of reprimand, suspend, or terminate teachers.*

❖ *We are a local control state*

❖ *The Department cannot discipline individual educators. The answers indicate what actions have been taken by school districts.*

❖ *We are in the process of our first certification revocation hearing.*

❖ *Staff discipline is handled by district and by the Teacher Standards and Practices Commission, not by the Dept of Education. TSPC has administrative rules requiring districts to report instances of "gross neglect of duty." All district/school staff involved in testing are made aware of this requirement and that testing improprieties may lead to disciplinary action by TSPC (potentially including loss of licensure or other sanctions).*

❖ *Schools/districts have imposed some of the above sanctions; however, the state has not.*

❖ *Suspension of license - limits on participation in administering the state assessment. Most actions are taken by local district*

16. **In the past three years, how many separate incidents have caused your state to take formal action (e.g., canceling test scores) due to a suspected or confirmed test security breach?**

Percentage

Response Count = 21

	Percentage
a. None	19.0
b. One	4.8
c. Two	4.8
d. More than two	71.4

C. What is Important/Worrisome to States

17. How concerned are you about each of the following types of test security breaches?	Response Count	Percentage Moderately or Very Concerned
a. Lost or stolen test booklets	22	63.6
b. Teachers coaching students before tests on specific questions	22	90.9
c. Teachers providing answers to students during testing	22	86.4
d. Teachers changing student responses after testing	22	72.7
e. Administrators changing student responses after testing	22	72.7
f. Students working together on the test in violation of testing rules	22	54.5
g. Students using technology (e.g., cell phones, PDAs) for cheating	22	81.8
h. Early test takers providing test questions and/or answers to later test takers	22	45.5
i. Test questions and/or answers being posted electronically	22	86.4

> **Other Areas of Concern (specified in Question # 17)**

❖ *Accommodations such as Read Alouds being used in such a way that allows students to know what other test takers answers are.*

❖ *Teachers allowing students to access unauthorized materials and internet during testing.*

❖ *Organized efforts to provide invalid responses related to test takers.*

❖ *Due to [our state's] adaptive online test which pulls from a pool of 18000 + items, the risk of teachers accessing/changing student responses after testing is minimized, as is the risk of exposure between students.*

18. Which statement best describes your state's test delivery mode?
Response Count = 22

		Percentage
a.	We test mostly in paper-pencil mode and plan to continue so.	9.1
b.	We test mostly in paper-pencil mode, but anticipate changing to computer-based testing.	54.5
c.	We test some students in paper-pencil mode and some by computer.	18.2
d.	We test most students on computers.	18.2

19. **Please describe your test security concerns, if any, specifically related to assessments being delivered by computer.**
Response Count = 12

> ❖ Expanded testing windows and testing across multiple states heightens security issues.
> ❖ The availability of searching the web to find answers to questions during the test and to differentially access various computer based tools that might aid some students and not be available to others.
> ❖ Copying memorable test items that are expensive to develop and posting them online or distributing them to other schools/students.
> ❖ We do have an option for grade 8 and grade 11 schools to administer the writen test on-line, and we offer a computer version of the science test for students who need accommodations.
> ❖ Security of student login information; educators logging into student tests to preview questions or change student responses.
> ❖ Ability to print or e-mail information, information stored in computer systems
> ❖ Hacking into computers, the secure transfer of data, keystroke logging, technology failure leading to partial completion of testing, verifying identity of students
> ❖ Posting test items on the internet, students who test early in the extended testing window needed due to limited # of computers in schools sharing the test items with other students
> ❖ Students copying from proximal computers.
> ❖ Students seeing the same items or passages at different times throughout the school year. There is a difference between fixed form assessments delivered by computer versus computer adaptive assessments delivered via computer.
> ❖ Student coaching during test administration (e.g., teacher leading students through instructional strategies or otherwise leading students to the correct answer).
> ❖ Our concerns center around student sharing of secure questions seen during their session with later test takers, teacher inappropriate assistance during test sessions, and teacher use of specific secure test items in review sheets.

20 **In order to improve test security in your state, how important is each of the following?**

	Response Count	Percentage Somewhat or Very Important
a. Improved policies and procedures	22	90.9
b. Better training	22	86.4
c. Greater oversight of test administration	22	86.4
d. Better budgets for test security work	22	81.8
e. Changes in state legislation	21	38.1
f. Assistance from outside individuals or organizations	22	50.0
g. An objective, third-party evaluation or audit of your state's test security measures	22	59.1

> ➢ **Other Important Areas Needing Improvement (specified in Question # 20)**

> ❖ A specified plan of action approved at the highest levels of administration.
> ❖ Consideration of other alternatives for investigations such as state police conducting the investigations.
> ❖ Developing methods that allow to investigate test security breaches in computer adaptive testing by investigating data

21. If you needed to take an action (e.g., canceling an examinee's score) due to a test security breach, how concerned would you be about the following?

	Response Count	Percentage Moderately or Very Concerned
a. Insufficient evidence	22	77.3
b. Potential legal action by or on behalf of the examinee	22	54.5
c. The gravity/stigma of an accusation of cheating	22	54.5
d. Lack of precedent	22	50.0
e. Lack of agreed upon procedures	22	40.9
f. Lack of formal authority	22	31.8

> **Other Concerns about Taking Action (specified in Question # 21)**

- ❖ *Lack of formal documentation of consequences.*
- ❖ *Extent of the test security breach involving other classes or students of that teacher*

D. What Should be in the TILSA Test Security Guidebook

22. On the topic of Prevention, would the following information be important to be included in the Guidebook?

		Response Count	Percentage **Yes**
a.	Standards for each phase of the process of developing and implementing state assessment programs (paper-pencil as well as computer-based assessments)	22	86.4
b.	Resources available to states	22	95.5
c.	Sample checklists for each phase of assessment	22	90.9
d.	Guidelines for performing security audits	22	100.0
e.	Staffing and training modules	22	90.9
f.	Case studies of successful implementation of "best practices"	22	86.4

> **What else should be included on Prevention?**

❖ *Sample vignettes... do help people think about what is and what is not cheating.*

❖ *Examples and non-examples of inappropriate practices*

❖ *Information regarding analysis of responses which indicate irregularity; criteria for determination of irregularity*

❖ *It is very important to make a distinction between computer delivered CATs and computer delivered fixed form assessments. It would also be important to point out how the consortia (Smarter Balanced and PARCC) can use and apply the information and guidelines provided in the Guidebook.*

23. On the topic of Detection, would the following information be important to be included in the Guidebook?

		Response Count	Percentage **Yes**
a.	Types of data forensics approaches that are available, and strengths and weaknesses of each	22	100.0
b.	How to prepare schools for the use of data forensics analyses	22	81.8
c.	Sources of training and information	22	100.0
d.	Model communication program, including presentation material (e.g., PowerPoint)	22	90.9
e.	Case studies of uses being made of data forensics information	22	90.9
f.	Legal issues regarding the collection and use of data forensics information regarding possible testing misbehaviors	21	95.2

> **What else should be included on Detection?**

❖ *How to prepare LEAs for the use of data forensics analyses.*

❖ *Keep knowledge about cheating incidents/methods/responses/detection proprietary.*

❖ *Development of new data forensics methods and analyses which can be applied to "adaptive" testing. It would also be important to point out how the consortia (Smarter Balanced and PARCC) can use and apply the information and guidelines provided in the Guidebook.*

❖ *Possible ongoing listserve for new innovations in detection*

24. On the topic of Follow-Through Activities, would the following information be important to be included in the Guidebook?

		Response Count	Percentage Yes
a.	Potential roles for state level staff, school district staff and possible outside agencies in an investigation	22	100.0
b.	A model Investigations Kit with sample interview guides, forms, timelines, and suggested allocation of responsibilities	22	95.5
c.	Timelines for planning and carrying out investigations	22	90.9
d.	Special communication considerations for follow-through activities	22	90.9
e.	Case studies of follow-through investigations	22	90.9

➢ **What else should be included on Follow-Through Activities?**

❖ *A sample of a complete security plan highlighting especially detection and possible consequences for students, teachers, test administrators, school/district/charter administrators, as well as outside "civilians".*

❖ *It would also be important to point out how the consortia (Smarter Balanced and PARCC) can use and apply the information and guidelines provided in the Guidebook.*

John F. Olson, Ph.D.
Olson Educational Measurement & Assessment Services

John F. Olson is President of the consulting business he founded in 2006, *Olson Educational Measurement & Assessment Services (OEMAS)*, which provides technical assistance and support to states, school districts, the U.S. Department of Education, Ministries of Education in other countries, CCSSO, Caveon Test Security, testing companies, researchers, and others. He has more than 30 years of experience providing consulting on a variety of measurement and statistical issues for international, national, state, and local assessment programs. Dr. Olson also currently serves as senior partner for the *Assessment Solutions Group* (ASG), which he co-founded in 2008. The mission of ASG is to help states and local districts maximize value throughout the assessment procurement and implementation process. Previously, he has served as Vice President for Psychometrics and Research Services at Harcourt Assessment, Director of Assessment for CCSSO and the SCASS projects, Deputy Director of the Center for Education Assessment at American Institutes for Research (AIR), Senior Research Scientist with the Education Statistics Services Institute (ESSI), and in a number of leadership roles for NAEP at the Educational Testing Service (ETS). Dr. Olson holds a Ph.D. in educational statistics and measurement from the University of Nebraska - Lincoln.

John Fremer, Ph.D.
Caveon Consulting Services, Caveon LLC

John Fremer is President of Caveon Consulting Services and a Founder of Caveon Test Security, a company started in 2003 that helps testing companies, test sponsors, military and government agencies, and others prevent and detect test fraud, including cheating and test piracy. Dr. Fremer has 50 years of experience in the field of test publishing, including management level positions at ETS and The Psychological Corporation/Harcourt. He is a Past President of the National Council on Measurement in Education (NCME) and a former editor of the NCME journal *Educational Measurement: Issues and Practice*. He also served as President of ATP and of the Association for Assessment in Counseling (AAC). He was co-chair of the Joint Committee on Testing Practices (JCTP) and of the JCTP work group that developed the *Code of Fair Testing Practices in Education*. Dr. Fremer is a co-editor of *Computer-Based Testing: Building the Foundations for Future Assessments* (2002, Erlbaum) and co-editor of *The Handbook of Test Security* with a scheduled publication date of March 2013. Dr. Fremer was the lead author of the Test Security chapter of the *Operational Best Practices in State Assessment* document issued in 2010 by ATP and the CCSSO. He received the 2007 ATP Career Award for Contributions to Measurement and a Career Recognition Award in 2012 from the National Association of Test Directors. Dr. Fremer has a Ph.D. from Teachers College, Columbia University, where he studied with Sam Ball, Robert L. Thorndike and Walter MacGinitie.